The Novels of V.S. Naipaul
Immigrant-Angst Across the Seven Seas

The Novels of V.S. Naipaul

Immigrant-Angst Across the Seven Seas

by

Dr. Rishi Pal Singh

Associate Professor of English,

Post Graduate Department of English Studies & Research

Govt. Kamala Raja Girls Postgraduate (Autonomous) College

Gwalior (M.P.)

ADHYAYAN

ADHYAYAN PUBLISHERS & DISTRIBUTORS

New Delhi-110002

Published by
ADHYAYAN PUBLISHERS & DISTRIBUTORS
4378/4B, 105, J.M.D. House, Murari Lal Street
Ansari Road Darya Ganj, New Delhi - 110002
Ph.: 011-23263018, 011-23277156, Fax: 23280028
Email: adhyayanpublishers@yahoo.com

The Novels of V.S. Naipaul

Edition 2011
ISBN 978-81-8435-250-4

Printed in India

Published by Harish Chandra Yadav for Adhyayan Publishers & Distributors. Delhi. Laser Typesetting at Jain Computers and Printed at Tarun Offset Printers. Delhi

Dedicated to

My bosom friend

'OSHIN'

Who has died and departed but
Still his presence in my life makes me feel
the Resonance of God

Preface

Disintegration, exile, alienation, loss of values and quest for identity are the terms often applied for defining the experiences of the people of the Third World nations and in the aftermath of imperialism, the miserable societies of these third-rated countries are struggling to achieve their economic self-reliance, political stability and a national self-esteem which are yet beyond their reach. In such a chaotic situation the expatriates in general and the indentured Asians in particular are in a gruesome predicament since they are already under the curse of exile and dereliction; their ancestral identity is a dead-ended past and original culture has disintegrated and dissolved amidst the alien surroundings. No doubt, the condition of these half-made slave societies marooned on alien lands has become more miserable in the recent whirlwind of globalization and the throes of marginalization, deracination, disintegration and nowhereness have become more painful and unbearable than ever. Frankly speaking, their crisis is neither exclusively economic nor purely political because these are only two aspects of a larger crisis that, at heart, is civilizational since they have undergone a colossal loss of their past and do lack any substitute identity at all. This traumatic transition and desperate struggle for existence in limbo rendered these poverty-ridden Indians agnostics and unbelievers haunted by an indefinable fear-psychosis of non-entity. Consequently, these uprooted people suffer from an existential despair and a deep penetrating sense of *'no land's men'*.

Sir Vidiadhar Surajprasad Naipaul, the Nobel Laureate of Indian origin, has a distinctive and conspicuous position in the galaxy of the Diaspora writers. Having a terrifying passion for truth, even if it is sour, Naipaul has undoubtedly emerged as a relentlessly truthful delineator of the gruesome maladies of the immigrants and his novels present a true picture of the indentured Indians—rather Asians in their floatsam existence as derelict peoples in the wilderness of the modern world. These people, including the author himself, are on a perpetual journey away from their origin but there is not any arrival anywhere—so a pointless one. Being a twice exiled writer—coming from the indentured Indian community in Trinidad and living in the English world of his choice and adaption¯ Naipaul situates his novels in both the colonial as well as the postcolonial situations to record a perspective account of the complexities of the expatriates without any inhibition or reservation. With a literary career of spanning half a century and more than30 genre defying books to his credit, Naipaul's entire literature is a spiraling round and round the expatriate themes which are central to his creative effusion. Naipaul argues his ways through the treacherous alleys of the heterogeneous societies of the immigrants and by making an admixture of facts and fiction in his stories he exposes their wounds and ailments with a surgeon-like objectivity and dexterity.

This research work is an honest attempt to analyze the novels of this audacious writer to explores the prevailing socio-cultural confusion, fluidity of life, moral vacuum and emotional aridity in these people whose presence on the alien land is merely an accident and wreckage of history and who are desperately searching for a foothold and niche. Though there are a host of modern writers who deal with the cross-cultural themes, few would deny the fact that Naipaul is a highly defiant and audacious, innovative and mysteriously enchanting delineator of the wounds and ailments of the

Indian Diaspora in the postcolonial literature the world over in any language. This study is an attempt to probe deep into the soul and psyche of these uprooted people amidst the challenges which are of global dimensions and have been satirically—rather sardonically depicted by this literary giant who is Indian by ancestry, Trinidadian by birth and English by sense and sensibility. The study has also made an objective analysis of the intimate experiences and influences that went in shaping the splendid vision and sensibility of this literary giant who, though seems Anglophile yet maintains a surgeon-like objectivity while dissecting the mutual grievances and maladies of the colonized as well as the colonizers. The study presents a righteous assessment of his works that have otherwise provoked and enraged the people of the Third World and have received a chiding sneer from them.

Actually the Indians' experiences in the West Indies are of a cheating contract—a long sea journey, an aimless isolation with no hope of redress are no less than the Negro experiences there—of enslavement, of servitude and of the loss of their racial identity and ancestral past. The exiled status made these immigrants to succumb to the conglomeration of different cultural, religious and ethnic groups which created utter confusion in their minds and an emotional vacuum in their hearts. The corrosive influence of the materialism and disgusting desolation has resulted in widespread despair and fear-psychosis lest their identity be swallowed in such oppressive situations and herein lies the root cause of their anxiety and despair. Being a third generation expatriate Indian in Trinidad, Naipaul sprang from the exiled Hindu community and spent his childhood and formative years of adolescence by witnessing the painful breakdown of the socio-cultural heritage of his community there. So Naipaul is truthful and emphatic in the delineation of the lived experiences of himself as well as of his own people. It is equally noticeable that Naipaul picturises even their craving for some substitute identity, integrity or authenticity to replace their fluidity of life and existential despair. The prolific novelist highlights that fragmentation and desolation, both at the macrocosmic level of the societies as well as the microcosmic level of the individual relationships, act as aggressive deterrents to stability, integrity and growth in the era of globalization. Moreover, through relentless and truthful assertions a meaningful rejuvenation of the expatriate society is also aimed at as Naipaul's works give a shock treatment, which, the novelist believes, is essential to pull them out of their complacency and make them shoulder their responsibilities towards themselves in the present scenario of the world. Most amazingly and fortunately, Naipaul himself has procured a wisdom to look on life, on death, on man and on all human existence in modern world as a mystery which is equally baffling to each and every man and this self-ordained realization has harnessed him with a Ulysses-like power of looking at and accepting the world in a new perspective without any grudge or complain at all.

This study deals with the presentation of the immigrants' endless woes and sorrows in Naipaul's novels and covers only those novels that focus on the expatriate community and demonstrate an immediate and obvious concern with the former colonized societies. For the same reason the novel *'Mr. Stone and the Knight's Companion,'* which portrays the English middle-class life, has been excluded from this analyses. Naipaul's output of non-fiction is also prolific and closely interlinked to his fiction, but those works have only been taken up for discussion wherever considered relevant for the thematic purpose and, if needed, references have also been drawn. Since the purpose of this study is to explore the problems of the former colonized people, especially the immigrants an attempt has been made to approach the novels primarily from the point of view of the themes, while at the same time attempting to maintain their chronological order.

The title of the book itself defines the scope as well as purpose of my research endeavour. The work has been divided into seven chapters as : 1. Introduction—V.S.Naipaul: A Decolonised Citizen of the World, 2. Making of a Writer:

Ordeal and Evolution of Naipaul's Vision and Sensibility, 3. Cultural Disintegration and Immigrants' Quest for Identity in Limbo, 4. Postcolonial Chaos and Paradox of Freedom and Power in the Third World Nations, 5. Fluidity of Life and Existential Despair in the Ex-Colonies, 6. Ironical Effacement of Diaspora Identity Across the Seven Seas, 7. Summing-Up. The first chapter presents a brief sketch of the life of V.S.Naipaul and also his decolonized profile as a truly liberated citizen of the modern world. In the second chapter I have attempted an objective analysis of the formative influences on V.S.Naipaul's vision and voice. All the pleasures and pains of the struggle of this literary giant during his ordeal and the consequent evolution of his unique vision and sensibility have been discussed to ascertain his attitude and mindset. The four core chapters 3, 4, 5 and 6 are self-explanatory of the matters discussed in them. I have explored here the various aspects of the immigrants- angst across the seven seas as articulated by the novelist progressively in his novels. Chapter 7 is an attempt to summarize the findings of this study to assess the contribution of this high profile novelist to the expatriates' world as well as to the humanity at large amidst the complexities of the modern time in the light of the subject. The textual quotations and the critical opinions of other critics and scholars are chapter-wise marked with serial numbers for the purpose of convenience and are clearly explained in the end of each chapter, but they are strictly adhered to the publications referred in the footnotes and Bibliography. A well-planned Bibliography has been given at the end of the book so as to facilitate the comprehensive reading of this book as well as for further extensive readings by the students.

This preface will remain incomplete if I fail to acknowledge my indebtedness to those scholars, relatives, friends and literary agencies that have extended every possible help during my study for this research work and writing of this book. I'm obliged to many critics acknowledged and many more who have remained unacknowledged whose ideas have helped me immensely in forming and substantiating the views expressed in this work. It is a pleasure to record my gratitude to all the people and institutions that have made this work possible. I am really grateful to Professor O.F. Budholia, Head of the Department of English, Government Kamala Raja Girls Post Graduate (Autonomous) college, Gwalior for the encouragement and valuable suggestions during this research pursuit. I am equally thankful to all faculty members of the English Department i.e. Prof. Savita Shrivastava, Miss. Preeti Shrivastava, Dr. Beena Laad, Dr. Sonia Singh Kushwah, Dr. Lata Mishra, Dr. Charu Chitra and Dr. M.K. Sharma for taking a keen interest in my work and helping me in every possible way.

I am also grateful to the librarians and staff members of the British Council Library New Delhi, Sahitya Academi Library New Delhi, Delhi University Library New Delhi, Aligarh Muslim University Library Aligarh, Meerut University Library Meerut, Jiwaji University Library Gwalior and Central Library, Anna University Chennai and, of course, the Library of Govt. K.R.G. Post Graduate College Gwalior. I must acknowledge my indebtedness to all those who have directly or indirectly helped me during this research work. Most remarkably, I convey my sincere thanks and gratitude to the University Grants Commission C.R.O. Bhopal for providing me the financial support in the form of MinorResearch Project on this theme.

I will always remain indebted to my three true friends who are indispensible in my life and so are valuable assets for me and my gratitude will best be expressed here by leaving them unnamed. They are the positive forces always inspiring me to excel and be creative and whenever I achieve something worthwhile they feel a greater happiness than experienced even by me. I do honestly acknowledge the persistent cooperation, tireless patience and inspiring innocence of my wife Smt. Kalpana Singh Gurjar who helped me in giving a concrete shape to the dream of writing this book. I feel pleasure in expressing my special thanks and love to my curious children Aayush and Mudita who have rigorously imbued me with a zeal to complete this work. I will be failing in my sincerity if I do not acknowledge my indebtedness to my reverent father Choudhary Hukum Singh and love pouring mother Smt. Narayani Devi whose blessings and simplicity have always been great spiritual power to guide and inspire me towards ideal goal in my life. Above all, I acknowledge the power of ALMIGHTY with a complete submission to His Will for steering me out of all the hurdles and difficulties in my life and, so also, during the course of this research pursuit.

Rishi Pal Singh

Contents

	Preface	vii
1.	*Introduction* V.S. Naipaul: A Decolonised Citizen of the World	1
2.	The Making of a Writer: Ordeal and Evolution of V.S. Naipaul's Vision and Sensibility	19
3.	Cultural Disintegration and Immigrants' Quest for Identity in Limbo	41
4.	Postcolonial Chaos and Paradox of Freedom and Power in the Third World Nations	78
5.	Fluidity of Life and Existential Despair in the Ex-Colonies	115
6.	Ironical Effacement of Diaspora Identity Across the Seven Seas	143
7.	Summing-Up	172
	Bibliography	193
	Index	203

1

Introduction

V.S. Naipaul: A Decolonised Citizen of the World

"I didn't know who I was."[1]

– V.S. Naipaul

An emerging feature in the post World War II period is the flourishing of the expatriate literature. All the colonized countries, enslaved either by England or by any other power, were gradually liberated and in the postcolonial era they have emerged with new dimensions and stature in all the walks of life including their literature also. Industrialization, advance of technology, novel modes of transport and migration have created new phenomena of disintegration, exile, alienation, disorder and a loss of identity. In the whirlwind of globalization the people of Third World nations are desperately engaged in searching their potential for a political and economic growth on the one hand and for a social stability and search for identity on the other. No doubt, in the aftermath of imperialism the miserable societies of these countries were already struggling for their economic self-reliance when the subtle process of globalization exposed their people to new challenges which they find difficult to grapple with. Obviously, the condition of the half-made societies in the slave countries compelled many promising and ambitious intellectuals to find their shelter in the western countries. Exodus from the underdeveloped Third World countries to the developed western countries is a commonly observed phenomenon and this they did for widening their horizon and gaining new opportunities in the Metropolitan centers. Ages ago, it was the lure for gold which set off a chain of sailors and explorers from the west like Columbus and Sir Walter Raleigh towards the least developed lands of the world. In the postcolonial times there is a reversal of these journeys and the advanced west fascinates the intellectuals and academic explores from the Third World nations. The expatriate writers thus are the new Columbuses sailing out from the backward countries to the advance western countries to recreate a new world as the process of decolonization has led them to vociferous assertions of their thoughts through literature. As a result a new content entered the mainstream of traditional English literature, mingled and merged with it and slowly led to a disregard for the recognition of a monolithic corpus of English literature. On the derogatory delineation of the colonies the intellectuals of the Third World were deeply hurt and they started mobilizing the subjugate people to rise up against and to overthrow the imperial hegemony. They made literature as the medium to prepare the ground and after a long preparation it was in the early twentieth century that the colonized elites, on their own lands or expatriates in western countries, appropriated the language and literature of the colonies. This literature sought to subvert the western dominance and also to recover the suppressed identity of the colonized subjects.

The postcolonial literature primarily deals with the experiences of the colonized people and in the context of the Caribbean countries too, there has been substantial contribution to it. The jubilations, aspirations, hopes, fears, anxieties and crises of the expatriate writers coming from the newly independent countries revitalised the English literature making it very vibrant with disparage stream – truly postmodern.

As every age nurtures literature which favours and inspires it, the postcolonial literature of the twentieth century written by the expatriates depicting the predicament of the Diaspora also has its distinguished features. In the postcolonial time several of these writers who live as expatriates in England or America and contribute to the body of the expatriate literature, show a concern for their exiled status, incessant travels, displacement, alienation, rootlessness and homeless ness. An expatriate may live abroad without acquiring citizenship there like a resident alien as Aldous Huxley did in U.S.A., or one may acquire citizenship and home but may still experience the social and cultural vacuum of an exile. V.S. Naipaul, in spite of his 56 years settlement in England, belongs to this category. His prolonged stay and marriage with an English lady could not free him from his persistent feeling of rootless ness. The wider process of the experience of Diaspora has various moods woven into it and the expatriate literature aims at an exposition of such perceptions and experiences.

Sir Vidiadhar Surajprasad Naipaul, the Nobel Laureate of India, has a distinctive and conspicuous position in the galaxy of the Diaspora writers. With a literary career of spanning half a century and more than 30 genre-defying books to his credit, Naipaul's entire contribution to literature is a spiraling round and round the expatriate themes which are central to his creative effusion. He is rather notorious and merciless but a truthful story teller who argues his ways through the treacherous alleys of the half-made colonial societies of the Third World and whose forceful imagination is inseparable from the wreckage of history. No doubt, he is a writer with Eurocentric sensibility but he is defiant and audacious in his observations and assertions about the immigrant's life in alien environment. Having a terrifying passion for truth, even if it is sour, Naipaul spares neither the colonisers nor the colonised while exposing the naked wounds on expatriates' mind and heart which are beyond all hopes of healing or redresses. The saga of the fluid life and existential despair of the immigrants is intensely passionate and moving and therefore, his works simultaneously delight and astonish his readers.

None can deny the truth that V.S. Naipaul, with London as the base of his creativity, has contributed voluminously and qualitatively to the mainstream of British fiction. It is equally well known that London remained the land of his literary exercises and craftsmanship but it is his journeys to various countries including Trinidad—his birth place, and India—his ancestral homeland, which have given him stuff for his literary works. Indeed, Naipaul's literature originated form his own odd suspicious situation; an uprooted and twice exiled writer Indian by ancestry, Trinidadian by birth and English by temperament, writing for an English audience about non-English situations and characters who talk their own sort of English. As a merciless provocateur and somewhat narcissistic writer, Naipaul constantly challenges the received wisdom of time in dealing with the predicament of the expatriate people in the colonial and postcolonial world. In his ruthless style he dissects the historical perspectives of the cultures through a large number of his fictional and non fictional works. This literary giant is never restricted by national boundaries; his freedom is accentuated by his existential status as an exile who doesn't miss home. When he remembers any region of the world there is no nostalgia; when he talks about his ancestry there is no sentimentality; and when he slices up any country or culture he never bothers about his criticism. For example, the Indians were enraged at his merciless observations exposing the disgusting truths of this country in his works like *'An Area of Darkness' (1964)' 'India: A Wounded Civilization' (1979)* and *'India; A Million Mutinies Now' (1990)*. But, by mentioning India in his Nobel acceptance statement as the land of his ancestors along with Britain the country of his adoption, Naipaul has delighted his readers more in India than anywhere else. Irrespective of all humiliating articulation of India in his works, Naipaul, on this occasion, received immense appreciation from this country of his forefathers. Indian newspapers, who were aggressively chiding him for his attitude in *'An Area of Darkness'*, now vied with each other to claim Naipaul as the second Indian to win the Nobel Prize for literature after R.N. Tagore.

The fate of numerous writers from the Third World countries including West Indies and India also fluctuated between fame and haziness in the world of literature. From 1960 onwards the West Indian writers grew in number, dimension and stature. For example, the novelists like Andrew Salkey, Michael Anthony, Austin Clarke and Garth St. Omer have also emerged with their considerable contributions. Some novelists like Denis Williams and Orlando Patterson have become famous for their single novels. Poetry also flourished and Dereck Walcott, the winner of the Nobel Prize, came from St. Lucia, Wilson Harois and Mittalholzer from Guyana and Jean Rhys from Dominica. Wayne Browne, Anthony Meneill, Mervyn Mornis and Dannis Scott are some more poets writing with considerable success. Several of these writers live as expatriates in England or America and they are filled with a concern for their homeland and share the wider themes of rootlessness, search for identity and authenticity. They are overwhelmed and agonised due to the constant changes and flux amidst fluidity of life and the crumbling down of their redundant, hazy and distant past. The West Indian literature is one of the major groups today in New Literatures written in English Language and V.S. Naipaul is an extraordinarily important name in bringing this literature to its full blossoming. Another Nobel Prize winner Dereck Wallcott has, of late, become celebrated but he belongs to the world of poetry. However, George Lamming, V.S. Naipaul's brother Shiva Naipaul and some other West Indian writers take their place along with other celebrated Third World writers like Vikram Seth, Salman Rushdie, Anita Desai, Kamala Das and Kiran Desai from India, Yasmine Goonaratne from Australia and Chinua Achebe from Africa.

V.S. Naipaul is, undoubtedly, one of the high profile and most towering figures of the postcolonial literature the world over in any language. He is innovative, mysteriously interesting and relentlessly truthful delineator of the hopes and fears, aspirations and frustrations and anxieties and challenges experienced by the immigrants in the alien surroundings. More interestingly, Naipaul, though a little Narcissistic, constantly challenges the received wisdom of time in his treatment of the themes of rootlessness, alienation, deracination, and nowhere ness in the wilderness of modern world. As an author of a large number of fictional and non-fictional works, he continues to surprise, excite, provoke and even move his readers at every turn of his literary voyage across the world. A major portion of his life can be constructed from Naipaul's numerous books which belong to various literary genres: sometimes they even blend and become a mingled medley of disparate strains.

V.S. Naipaul was born on 17th August, 1932 in a small family of Indian immigrants atChaguanas in central Trinidad. Chaguanas has been referred to as the peasant paradise which then consisted of 1452 inhabitants and only 43 ratable buildings. He was born in Lion House, home of Capildeo family whose seventh daughter Broptie was married to his father in 1929. The Capildeo were wealthy people with status but Naipaul's father was struggling and poor journalist, although, one of the first Indian rather Asian in Trinidad to write about their own community. The house of Capildeo has been described by Naipaul as:

> "My mother's family house in Chaguanas was a well known big house. It was built in the North Indian style. It had ballustrated roof services and the main terrace was decorated at either end with a statue of a rampant lion."[2]

The Capildeo house, in some respects, resembles 'the Hanuman House' of Tulsi family in *'A House for Mr. Biswas'*. Naipaul had three sisters one of them just two years older than himself like Anand in '*A House for Mr. Biswas*'. The child Naipaul spent just two years at Chaguanas Government School which his father had attended 22 year earlier. In 1938 his father had to move to Port of Spain as a city reporter and the boy was shifted to Tranquility Boys School there. Later, reflecting on this change in his life, Naipaul wrote that his response was a pleasant one and he liked the change. He writes about the significance of this move to the Port of Spain:

> "In Chaguanas, the family had been at the centre of a whole network of Hindu reverences. People were always coming to the Chaguanas house to pay their respects, to issue invitations, or to bring gifts of food. Here we were alone. Unsupported by that Chaguanas world, with no one outside to instruct us in our obligations, even to ourselves, or own internal reverences began to go; our Hindu system began to fail."[3]

However, Naipaul did well in his studies and obtained the 3rd position in the exhibition examination and gained a free place at Queen's Royal College in Port of Spain. When he was only in the fourth form, he inscribed in his Kennedy's Revised Latin Premier ; a vow to escape from Trinidad within five years. The 'flight' which characterises the life of an expatriate as well as the sense of alienation started in Naipaul's life at a very early stage and he left Trinidad after six years of this resolution. In 1949 he won a Government Scholarship and opted to study at Oxford the long cherished place of Naipaul. In 1950 he returned to Queen's Royal College as a student teacher but left after six months to take up his place in University College Oxford. This was a second Diaspora in Naipaul's life—the journey to the Imperial Metropolis for education, exposure, opportunities and creativity. Writing about his going to Oxford, Naipaul states:

> "In 1949 I won a Trinidad Government Scholarship. These scholarships were meant to give a man a

> profession and they could last for seven years. I decided to use mine to do English at Oxford. I didn't want the degree, I wanted only to get away, and I thought that in three or four scholarship years at Oxford my talent would somehow be revealed and the books would start writing themselves."[4]

Naipaul's rejection of his birth place was circumscribed by the lack of opportunities in the colonial Trinidad which consisted of many social groups comprising heterogeneous people coming from distant races, religions and cultures and whose presence on the island was purely an accident of history. However, these islands proved to be the cradle for his initial identity as the son of the already exiled parents and also provided him material for first many books that established his reputation as a writer. Even in London Naipaul was not free from his weird and unpromising past in the slave society of the Colonial Trinidad. On the other hand, here also he experienced the agony of a lack of acceptance and belongingness. The young Naipaul found the Oxford students provincial, mean, impregnable and common. After getting a degree from Oxford in 1953 he returned to London and plunged deep into the adventure of writing. By this time he had lost his father and his family was in distress but he was audacious enough not to go back to Trinidad unless he became a writer. Even in London Naipaul was not free from the existential despair and felt lonely and miserable. Reiterating his deep sense of being adrift and alienated that followed him even in London, he writes:

> "I had dreamed of coming to England. But my life in England had been savourless and much of it mean. I had taken to England all the sadness of my colonial nerves and those nerves had more or less remained, nerves which in the beginning were in a good part also the nerves of youth and inexperience, physical and sexual inadequacy and of undeveloped talent. And just as once at home I had dreamed of being

> in England, so for years in England, I had dreamed of leaving England."[5]

He did experience strange metamorphosis in his personality and perception. Perhaps this enigmatic existence in limbo enkindled in Naipaul a wish to be a globally acknowledged writer in non-native language English. The early separation from the parents bred in him a deep sense of rootlessness, alienation and desolation that eventually sprouted into a rare faculty of literary imagination for extensive readings as well as a vision for creative endeavours. Strange things happened to Naipaul and this stress of dejection and insecurity in exiled life provided him a wild passion for creativity. The personal cognizance of Naipaul became a collective consciousness of the expatriates and got the emotional as well as the rational manifestation in his fictional and non-fictional works at large.

In 1955 he got a small part-time job in the B.B.C. to work on a half-weekly literary programme for the Caribbeans. He writes about it in *'Finding the Centre'* as:

> "The Caribbean service was on the second floor of what had been the Langham Hotel, opposite Broadcasting House. On this floor, the B.B.C. had set aside a room for people like me 'freelancers'–to me then not a word suggesting freedom and velour, but suggesting only people on the fringe of mighty enterprise, depressed and suppliant class."[6]

Naipaul utilized these formative years for rigorous study and for inculcating his own craftsmanship as a writer. He writes in this connection : **"All mythical land faded, and in the big city I was confined to a smaller world than I had ever known. I became my flat, my desk, my name."**[7] Then he also worked as a reviewer for *'The New Statesman'* and *'The Daily Telegraph'* (1956-1960). In spite of these professional assignments Naipaul could not find peace with himself since deep within this man there was an incessant agony to find his own literary voice, his own narrative form and his own identity as a writer. Determined and destined to become a writer Naipaul evolved his own defiant literary vision and voice. He himself reiterates his determination to become a writer as no other occupation suited his unyielding temperament and restless soul.

> "I began to write, I am afraid, for no other reason than because I thought it would be nice to be a writer. I had nothing to say. My vision of writing and the life it meant was so childish really writing articles and having them collected and all this sort of rubbish – which has nothing to do with writing. One began with this very romantic vision of the writer as a free gifted, talented creature admired person – with writing as a kind of social and cultural and sexual attribute... In fact, writing is just a sort of disease, a sickness. It is a form of incompleteness, it is a form of anguish, it's despair."[8]

Actually, Naipaul was in search of a new promising direction in his life and was also apprehensive of a probable crisis in creativity. With an optimistic attitude to solve this enigma, Naipaul, though living mainly in London, traveled frequently in the West Indies, Asia, North and South America and Africa. As he traveled – physically or mentally—to the dark interiors of the Caribbean islands, India and other countries of the Third World he made a remarkable progress as a writer publishing several books and winning numerous awards. Works of Naipaul are the fictional narratives as well as travelogues of the trampled histories of a world let down by competing ideas of liberation. In 1955, Naipaul married Patricia Anne Hale, a fellow student but he never mentions her in his books. However, Paul Theroux[9] has observed that she is behind every word Naipaul writes. In spite of all assumptions one thing is quite apparent that Naipaul's marriage to an English lady and even long stay in England could not erase the deep rooted impressions of his colonial background and he could still think that he was an 'outsider' in England. Often nodding off with the electric heater on, he would wake up to a nightmare that he was still in tropical Trinidad. In this way, though Naipaul made London the base for his creative pursuits, he travelled across the world and his travels gave exuberance to his talent by enriching him for writing unsurpassed books. Moreover, in accordance with his resolution to become a writer, he travelled with no other purpose except gratifying his restless soul with the first hand observation of different countries and that too, without any bias and without making any commitment to any land for his final identity. For example, when he travelled to the West Indies he went there not so much as a Hindu but as a product of Oxford University and so returned soon to his centre in England. Indeed, Naipaul found himself in an odd suspicious situation; an uprooted and twice exiled writer dealing with the predicament of the expatriates on alien lands. He initiated his creative works by writing about the inevitable collapse of the insulation on the East Indian society in West Indies and how the large scale deracination and disintegration has been caused by the imperial processes in the half-made salve societies. There is a regret for what the exiled Indians have lost in the West Indies, when it became irrelevant in the westernised set up of these underdeveloped colonies. The outcome of his one visit to West Indies was his travel book *'The Middle Passage'* (1962). There is also a vivid description of the tragedy of disintegration of the Hindu community on the colonial island because he knew it more intimately than to the English community of London. The writer proclaimed this truth about himself in 1958 as:

> "I live in England and depend on an English audience. Yet I write about Trinidad and more particularly the Indian community there. Few novels have been written about Trinidad and I can not deny that this gives me some advantages. There is the additional advantage that Trinidad society is so far unformed; ambitions are not uniform; the class structure is so fluid as to be almost non-existent; there is a vague urge to respectability but this can express itself in

> startling ways. Superficially, because of the multitude of races, Trinidad may seem complex but to anyone who knows it, it is simple, colonial Philistine society."[10]

Being a truthful artist, Naipaul was very sincere in realising that to write about English people only after living with them for a few years was not only difficult but unauthentic also. He felt himself comparatively close to his people in Trinidad as he made a confessional statement in the same article in clear words:

> "I feel, I know so little about England. I have met many people but I know them only in official attitude — the drink, the interview, the meal. I have a few friends. But that gives me only a superficial knowledge of the country and in order to write fiction it is necessary to know so much. We are not all brothers under the skin..... now I feel I can never hope to know as much about people here as I do about Trinidad Indians, people I can place almost as soon as I see them."[11]

Despite his own occasional assertions to be away from West Indies and the unseemly eagerness of Indians to label him as an Indian writer, Trinidad—the Caribbean island of his birth and adolescence formation—could not be erased and so has more claims to call him his own native. So far as India, the land of Naipaul's ancestral origin is concerned, his family's past roots are a part of historical darkness to him and when he did inquire further about this land — the very first attempt was a disaster — as far as his relationship with this country is concerned.

In accordance with his identification with the people of Trinidad, this prolific dissenter took the cudgel to delineate the predicament of the expatriates and their tireless search for stability and authenticity in the alien surrounding which, with the passage of time, now, has become their odd destiny and the truth of their existence. As Naipaul takes yet another step back to see more of the setting of his writings he does so by looking through many of the writers he has read carefully. The writers of the Caribbean origin like Derek Walcott, Samuel Selvon, Naipaul's own father Seeparsad, and Edgar Mittalholzar do inquire how every writer of the region has to find a way of going on, of not drying up, of overcoming the limitations of the place. Walcott got around it by fitting his island material to older foreign work; Selvon, after exhausting his Trinidad material, turned to the West Indian immigrants in London but still could not get beyond the limitations of his material; Seeparsad Naipaul, perhaps the first writer of the Indian Diaspora there, damaged his material when he tried to fit it to what he thought of as 'story' the trick ending say. V.S. Naipaul also considers this world as his material but infuses it with his own experiences and perceptions in the world of the imperial masters and this differentiates him from others. Moreover, he is relentless and unsparing in his articulation of the realities of the colonisers as well as the colonised without any inhibition or reservation at all.

From the artistic treatment of the East Indian society in Trinidad Naipaul's dedication to truthfulness is quite proved. It is obvious that he does not idealise the past of his people but at the same time believes that the present of any society or Individual can not be understood in isolation from their past. Therefore, his is a complete innovative voice representing the beginning of the great shift in ethnicity in English letters that could eventually see the triumph of such writers as Salman Rushdie, Ben Okrai, Zadie Smith, Arundhati Roy and Kiran Desai. Little of this would have been possible without the ground work put in by Naipaul whose craftsmanship is distinguished by his prose also that has startling clarity and precision, spare and deceptive simplicity and is penetratingly direct and honest at his best. S. Prasannarajan compliments Naipaul with these words:

> "Sir Vidiadhar Surajprasad Naipaul never ceases to astonish – with the intensity of his intellect, with the Englishness of his detachment, with the freedom

> of a way farer who doesn't have a past that is available to me, a past I can enter into and consider, but whose travels in the vandalised past of others have become some of the finest interventions in literature."[12]

Frequent travels to Trinidad, India, Africa and other parts of the world enriched him with a wide knowledge that provided him material to write his travelogues and other genre defying books. When he traveled to the West Indies for freshness he went there as a Eurocentric observer and the outcome of this travel was *'The Middle Passage'* (1962). Later, he traveled to India but found himself a misfit here and could not feel the power of the high sounding Indianness on his pulse. He returned to India again in 1975 and once again in the 1980s which enabled him to write the famous Trinity of Indian travels: *'An Area of Darkness'* (1965). *India : A Wounded Colonization'* (1975) and *'India : A million Mutinies Now'* (1990).

Once Naipaul had dreamt of settling down in India but he was totally disillusioned and returned to England a shattered person. For the next decades England became his home from where he traveled to distant countries frequently. London became his commercial centre, the centre of his literary activity like several other expatriate writers. For instance, Henry James, like Naipaul came to London from U.S.A. and settled down there and also pays similar glowing tribute to the city of London but both are not free form the ghost of their past and its images are articulated in their writings.

So far the question of his nationality is concerned Naipaul does not make any final commitment to any land. However he smells 'Eurocentric' and 'Anglophile' while expressing his views on different countries and his own relationship with them. His travelogues written on India depict Naipaul's attempt to understand his own past, to come to terms with it and to some extent, at least, to silence and mitigate his nagging awareness of not being too close to India but also not too far from her. For instance, at the initial stage of his career he made England his self-proclaimed home but in the recent years of the 21st century one could spot this literary giant in tweeds enjoying a quick drink with his Pakistani new wife Nadira in the bar of a Delhi hotel very often— India has emerged as his second home. Though Naipaul's intellectual bent is towards the western habits of thought, yet he could not throw away the burden of his past and his literary works have the involvement of the Indian people whether they deal with the Trinidadian society or the Indian one. His novels and travelogues mirror his own problem of being a writer thrown by destiny out in the void beyond Trinidad and the whole of the West Indies experience has been a long voyage in time and space and that too a pointless one.

To say the truth, Naipaul has stationed himself at a position from where he could have quite a good view of all the sides of the world and he maintains his narcissistic entity stranded above all the earthly overshadowing prides and prejudices. No doubt, Naipaul has been overpowered by the western metropolitan values and has lived all his writing career in England but that is to be acknowledged as the part of his world view. For example, if we consider him as an Indian writer in Diaspora only due to his ancestry, by the same logic, another Nobel winner Tonny Morrison would have to be called African writer because her ancestors were shipped from there to U.S.A. as slaves as Naipaul's grandfather had been indentured to the West Indies under the colonial rule. Actually Naipaul has been a serious traveler of the world and so can't pretend to be a writer who knows only one place because such a world view would be false. He himself says; **"All my life, I have had to think about ways of looking and how they alter the configuration of the world."**[13]

Thus Naipaul is a truthful delineator and even dissenter and he exposes the inner truths of both the colonisers and the colonised with same dexterity and to assign him any nationality is insufficient as well as unacceptable to him. Decades before either of them even dreamt of being a recipient of the Nobel, the young Caribbean poet Dereck Walcott, while interviewing Naipaul, had asked about his country and Naipaul's response **"I'm not a cricketer."**[14] conveyed his aversion to the game of cricket as much as his refusal to be labeled. The literary establishments took a while to catch up with the sharp edge of his relentless but truthful writings but, by now, he has become too towering a writer to be labeled as a man of any strict nationality at all. S. Prassanarjan in his article in *'India Today'* has realised this feature of Naipaul as a writer:

> "A master of details Naipaul places his novels in the real world and they reduce the distance between imagination and superb reportage. As a writer he is never restricted by national boundaries; his freedom is accentuated by his existential status as an exile who doesn't miss home."[15]

He is now an established writer of repute and has got the stature of a completely decolonized and international citizen of the world and the Naipaul cult has many fanatic followers and awestruck emulators all over the world. He has more than 30 books to his credit which cover a vast range— autobiography, fiction, travelogue, short story, journalism, criticism and that peculiar blend of all, a kaleidoscope of disparage streams—truly postmodern. From time to time limelight focuses on him; a bit of controversy, now and then but he has never bothered for his criticism or popularity rate anywhere. He has undoubtedly carved out a prominent place for himself in the mainstream of the postcolonial writers.

This research pursuit aims at exploring Naipaul's works for a righteous and judicious critique of the immigrant's predicament in alien lands where they are confronted with alien cultures. The stranded generations of the Indian Diaspora are picturised as still trying to find their feet across the seven seas. Naipaul's works revolve around this fear-psychosis and existential despair of these uprooted and second-rated people of the half-made societies in the Third World countries. I have made a sincere attempt at exploring Naipaul's important novels and travelogues with a purpose to probe into the deep recesses of the soul and psyche of the immigrants, especially the Indians, who are on a restless search for authenticity in their displaced existence. This book encompasses the broader perspective of V.S. Naipaul ashe has focused on the miserable predicament of their rootless ness, alienation and dereliction in alien lands where all their attempts at creating some sustainable substitute of identity end in nightmarish disillusionment and meaninglessness. This work presents an unbiased and objective analysis of Naipaul's main books from the point of view of immigrants angst and I hope it will prove a fruitful and justified interpretation for a righteous assessment of this giant author and his works that have, otherwise, provoked and enraged the people of the Third World and have received a lot of sneer from them.

References

1. V.S. Naipaul, 'Interview with Francis Wyndham;' *Sunday Times,* 10th Sept. 1968, p. 24.
2. ____________ *Finding the Centre,* (London : Penguin Books, 1965, Reprint 1988), pp. 52-53.
3. *Ibid.,* p. 31.
4. *Ibid.,* p. 36.
5. V.S. Naipaul, *The Enigma of Arrival* (London: Picador—an imprint of Pan Macmillan Ltd., 2002), p. 220.
6. ____________*Finding The Centre,* op.cit., p. 143.
7. V.S. Naipaul, *Times Literary Supplement,* London; 15 August, 1954.
8. ____________, *Critical Perspectives on V.S. Naipaul,* Edit by Robert D. Hammer. (London: 1979), 51-52.
9. Paul Theroux, *V.S. Naipaul: Modern Fiction Studies,*(Vol. 30, No. 3, Autumn, 1984), p. 452.
10. V.S. Naipaul, *Times Literary Supplement,* op. cit., p. 16.
11. *Idem.*

12. S. Prassanarajan, 'V.S. Naipaul: The Provocateur', '*India Today,(* Delhi: 10 Sept. 2007), p. 54.
13. V.S. Naipaul, 'Returning to the Centre' *The Sunday Express,* (New Delhi: 16 Sept. 2007), p. 3.
14. C. Vijaysree & T. Vijay Kumar, '*A House for Mr. Naipaul,*' IACLAL' s Newsletter, Jan. 2002, p. 1.
15. S Prassanarajan, op. cit., p. 54.

2

The Making of a Writer: Ordeal and Evolution of V.S. Naipaul's Vision and Sensibility

"Most imaginative writers discover themselves and their world through their works."[1]

– *V.S. Naipaul*

V.S. Naipaul has emerged as one of the elitist minorities in the twentieth century who took writing as their sole profession. There is no doubt in this fact that he is a prominent expatriate writer of the colonial experiences who situates his works in both colonial as well as post-colonial societies to articulate a perceptive account of the complexities inherent in such societies. His ordeal and moulding into a prolific writer has been explained from diverse angles practically in all his books. The record of his creative writing is varied and covers both fiction and non-fiction which complement each other and together become a live record of his progress as a writer par excellence. Much of his personal experiences as a displaced and exiled person have gone in enriching his sensibility and his creative writings, again and again, issue from his life and autobiographical material.

The long tenure of the imperial reign caused grave

damages to the soul and psyche of the people of the colonised countries and therefore in the post-independence era the Third World countries found themselves under the traumatic stress of instability and poverty. Elbaki Hermassi in his book *'The Third World Reassessed'* (1980) explains the nature of the crisis of these countries thus: **"It is neither purely political nor exclusively economic for the political and economic are only aspects of a larger crisis that is at the heart civilizational."**[2] For a people whose history and culture have been denigrated and who have been labeled as *'Whiteman's Burden'* the subjugation and its aftermath have inflicted unbearable pains and sufferings. More enraging became the glorification of the imperialism as a charity mission in the writings of Kipling and many other like—minded writers of the west. But we feel humiliated and intimately hurt when the writers of our own ethnicity and race upheld the colonialism as an essential presence in the underdeveloped countries. V.S. Naipaul belongs to such a school of writers who are disillusioned and disgusted with their homeland and *'An Area of Darkness'* (1964) is his most critical indictment of his ancestral country.

In such a complex situation it becomes imperative to analyse and assess the deep-rooted causes which led Naipaul to discard and shun India—the land of his ancestral origin, as well as Trinidad—the land of his birth and family. Derek Walcott wrote in a poem for *'Exiled Novelists'* as:

"You spit on your people,
Your people applaud,
Your former oppressors laurel you,
The thorns biting your forehead,
Are contempt disguised as concern
Still you can come home, now."[3]

Therefore, the critics who attribute him the nomenclature of a 'typical colonial Anglophile' on the basis of this severe indictment of the ex-colonies, must first make an objective study of the milieu and experiences which went in shaping

Naipaul's vision and sensibility and persuaded him to throw away his ancestral Indianness as redundant and ineffective burden of a dead past.

As a rule every human being imbibes various traits and trends from a number of phenomena. Naipaul has grown into a prolific writer with a splendid vision and voice from the rootless, fluid and insecure socio-cultural background. It will be in the fitness of things to have a bird's eye view of the multiple heritages in Naipaul's life and experiences which moulded him into a relentless, truthful and audacious literary giant of the present time. Naipaul was born in the West Indian island—Trinidad where he spent his childhood and formative years of adolescence in the colonial surroundings. He sprang from an uprooted minority of the traditional Hindus indentured there by the English colonial power from another colony—India long ago. The young Naipaul found himself in an odd indefinable situation where all the immigrants – Asian or African—were in a miserable predicament of rootlessness, dereliction, fluidity of life and existential despair on alien land. As a third generation Indian in Trinidad, he was never at ease with this subjugated identity and his agony and restlessness is quite obvious when he narrates in his works his childhood memories to render an account of his lived experiences in the colonial and ex-colonial Trinidad. He relates that the Indian experiences of the West Indies – a cheating contract, a long sea journey, an aimless dereliction, marginalization and isolation on alien land are no less than the Negro experiences there—enslavement, the middle passage and consequent disintegration.

Owing to their geographical separation in the countryside of Trinidad these Indians could hardly come in contact with the outside world and remained insular for a long time. Naipaul narrates that as a child he saw India scattered around him in physical objects – string beds, drums, mats, brass vessels and all the paraphernalia of the prayer room and all of these objects in varying state of extinction because there was no one with the caste skill to repair or replace them.

With the change of time India, their ancestral homeland also became a distant illusion for the new generation of these exiled immigrants and the cultural power of Indianness continued bickering and diminishing day by day. On the other hand their exposure to urbanization and Creole culture in the West Indies led them to cultural hybridization and gradually the insularity of these exiled East Indians was broken into. Thereafter, the painful process of the deracination of this stranded Hindu community happened on a fast pace amidst the heterogeneous social groups in the West Indies. Though the East Indians struggled a lot to preserve their socio-cultural identity, yet they were bound to ultimately succumb to the influences of the overpowering heterogeneous culture which reduced them to deracinated and anglicized immigrants and their Indianness was merely an inadequate and irrelevant past. To Naipaul this passage and exposure to the 'New World' marks a departure but not any arrival; it is the perpetual journey of his community in time and space and that too a pointless one. Moreover, the compromises that these stranded Indians born in exile and in a vulnerable environment are bound to make in order to forge some alternate identity for themselves are touchingly articulated by Naipaul in his fictional as well as non-fictional works.

Amidst such agonising situation Naipaul was desperate for his own identity and an indefinable fear of extinction haunted him from the very beginning of his life. For him the historical past of his family and community remained a part of darkness and also as imaginary as *Ramayan* until he personally came to experience the harsh realities of India when he made an attempt to establish his relationship with the renowned land of his ancestors. On the other hand, Trinidad, the land of his birth could provide him nothing worth holding because this colony had no great culture, no great economy, no great architecture, no memory of splendour and even no sense of oneness. The heterogeneous and fragmented society of Trinidad consisted of various races, religions and cliques and Naipaul could realise the fact that the Indian expatriates were no longer Asian but a part of the "New World" there. It is not only this experience that he, later, expresses in his oeuvre but also a revulsion, desolation and the tragedy of tenderness deprived of an outlet.

So Naipaul resolved to leave the West Indian island and in his self-ordained flight to England, he got a sort of refuge and exposure to greater fertile world away from the sordid existence in colonial Trinidad. In fact, his journey to England was 'escape' from the 'uncreative' environment of Trinidad with an intense passion for launching his career as a writer. Naipaul's sense of detachment can best be understood in the context of these conditions which were almost 'a second Diaspora' in his life. This was, in context of the long chronicle of his lineage, his second journey away from the group of the Indian people who have for a long time been marooned in the West Indies. This twice exiled status, though by choice, gave Naipaul a great opportunity for education and creativity but simultaneously distanced him from both his ancestral Indian as well as fortuitous Trinidadian backgrounds.

This ever-stranded status developed the personality of Naipaul into an audacious and comprehensively a non-aligned dissenter and his literary works reflect this liberated image through an admixture of facts and fiction at large. It is equally remarkable that rejecting the much prevalent thematic devices of sex, racial conflicts, and westerners' experiences in the colonial world, Naipaul took the challenge of writing about the idiosyncratic slave society, especially the expatriates lost in an alien landscape which never ceases to be unreal whether it is colonial or postcolonial time. The major themes that emerge in his works—fiction or non-fiction—are related to the problems of these colonised people in general and the immigrant Indians in particular. He is a superb prose writer of the day and the picturisation of alienation, identity crisis, paradox of freedom, existential pursuits and fluidity of life in the post colonial Third World is par excellence and true to the very core of facts. Actually Naipaul treats the material in a non-fictional form before going on to recast it into fiction and due to this his works invite a keen observation and sincere thinking about the nature of their writer's identity as an individual as well as a relentless giant writer of the time.

It is true that the commencement of Naipaul, the writer, was not an easy one because the West Indian tradition of writing did not exist. He writes in this connection, **"My material had not been sufficiently hallowed by a tradition."**[4] In the initial stage of his writings, Naipaul tried to resolve the creative crisis by recreating the stories of a Dickensonian novel in the Trinidadian context but the result was incongruous. Thereafter, he tried to utilize the Caribbean experiences for writing in English although he was not far away from his native country and lived only as an expatriate in England. This was a new formula, initiated by his father Seeparsad Naipaul in Trinidad and by others in different colonial countries. Naipaul makes a confession of it. "**A great deal of my vision of Trinidad had come straight from my father. Other writers are writing about rooted societies, his works showed me that one could write about another kind of society.**"[5] In reflecting on this peculiar situation and arriving at a conclusion, Naipaul uttered a truth of all time, "**Every writer is, on the long run, on his own; but it helps in the most practical way, to have a tradition. The English language was mine but the tradition was not.**"[6]

It was with this enigma is his mind that Naipaul had arrived in England and after the completion of his education, he came to London at the B.B.C. and got on to a real take off as a writer. In its freelancers' room, working to the rhythm of his typewriter, he launched on his writing pursuit reeling off his numerous memories back home in Port of Spain—Bogart Popo and the entire world of Trinidad started coming alive in his pages. In *'Finding the Centre'* (1965) he narrates how he sat at the typewriter with something like 'a monkey crouch,' typing his works. His fellow workers at the B.B.C., John Stockbridge and Andrew Salkey, frequently commented on his work.

Naipaul's problem, however, was not still solved. He failed to have the confidence to go on facing reviewers who regarded his writings as weird and fantasies when all the time he thought he was realistic in his description of Trinidad. The greatest hurdle was the lack of rapport with the channel of mass communication in which all others including Americans considered him British and the British regarded him as a foreigner. An added limitation was that he was a colonial; he could not write like an English or a French writer. Naipaul writers:

> "Because as a colonial, as I was to be spared knowledge, it was to live in an intellectually restricted world, it was to accept those restriction. So step by step, through seeking each time only to write another book, I eased myself into knowledge."[7]

Naipaul, thus, had to be a well-equipped person to be an effective writer. His problem as a colonial writer in an alien Metropolis, however well he could command the English language, was a genuine one. In the midst of this churning of ideas, he struck at a solution to write in English language for an immediate English audience but about the life in Trinidad. The thematic aspect created an impression of its being 'exotic' and failed to strike the right chord in the initial stages but Naipaul by now got an identity as' a new emerging writer: he arrived on the literary scene blazing new trail of his own. Once he started his career as a writer, Naipaul's gusto went on opening new horizons for his observation and analysis which is though severe but truthful and objective like that of an honest surgeon. On an average Naipaul wrote a book in every eighteen months and the number has gone beyond thirty by now. Naipaul's literary career may be conveniently classified into five successive stages. The first phase is the period of apprenticeship during which Naipaul draws upon the Trinidad memories and analyses the postcolonial scenario on the islands. Within a few years of his career Naipaul brought the first fruits of his craftsmanship to the light. His first book *'Miguel Street'* (Published in 1959) was written at this time although his first novel to be published was *'The Mystic Masseur' (1957)* followed by *'The Suffrage of Elvira' (1958)*. These early works are set in Port of Spain and the small villages of Trinidad like Chaguanas where the writer lived his early adolescent life. Here, he explores the world of postcolonial political scene and focuses on the rise of the West Indian politics. The description of Trinidadian milieu and flotsam existence of the peoples of various origins and races in the postcolonial upheaval is quite farcical, satiric and even sardonic but truthful without any reservation at all. *'The Mystic Masseur'* won the Llewelyn Rhys. Memorial prize for its humorous but vivid description of the expatriates and their political activities in the post independence era. *'The Suffrage of Elvira'* reveals an election scenario and describes the idiosyncratic behaviour of the people of the colonial existence on the arrival of democracy in Trinidad. *'Miguel Street'* is a volume of linked short stories bringing out the life of some common Trinidadian people and it won the Somerset award. *'A House for Mr. Biswas'* (1961) is his major work although written early in his life and it is an imaginative reconstruction of the immigrant Indians' experience in alien surroundings of Trinidad. This novel is rightly recognised as a prose epic of the postcolonial literature albeit a depressing one because after 1960 Naipaul's works got darkened with a sardonic cadence and unforgiving voice. In the world of literature this novel is hailed as a classic of modern fiction since the desperate struggle of its protagonist is symbolic manifestation of each and every uprooted individual's need to develop some authentic identity in the prevailing chaos of the post colonial Third World countries. By assuming the role of an official biographer of the rootless protagonist, Naipaul achieves a remarkable detachment that enables him to present the widespread predicament of the second and the third generation of the East Indian immigrants in hostile back ground of Trinidad. The novel portrays the struggle of Mr. Biswas, who is simultaneously heroic and absurd, and whose unrest and struggle is to carve a niche against the stifling existential pressures in the uncongenial environment. Moreover, the protagonist consistently referred as Mr. Biswas owes a great deal to the novelist's father who was a journalist and a failed writer, nevertheless a pioneer in the field of Diaspora writers. So this novel declared Naipaul's arrival at the literary firmament and also brought about the culmination of the first phase of his artistic development as a luminous man of letters. Here, it is noteworthy that the true value of these works can not be gauged in a vacuum and therefore to understand these otherwise warm and wryly amusing works of Naipaul, one must have a comprehensive knowledge of upheavals and flux in the postcolonial Trinidad. To evaluate Naipaul's artistic dexterity as well as his deep scrutinizing vision one must try to understand how he captures the political turmoil and all disintegrating socio cultural undercurrent at that time.

Naipaul struck a new ground when, on a travel scholarship, he visited Trinidad for the first time after he had left for England and the result of this travel was his travelogue '*The Middle Passage*' (1962). He visited his ancestral land India also with a great curiosity and wish to live there but was barely disillusioned and disheartened on looking at the harsh depressing realities of the land. He could not identify himself with India since his sensibility was a product of the New World. '*An Area of Darkness*' (1964) is his first travel book about his ancestral land and it is a disgusting narration of his first hand observations and experiences in India.

Naipaul's second phase started with his return to England and his decision to settle there. His first attempt at writing a novel based in an English setting '*Mr. Stone and the Knight's Companion*' (1963) though won the Hawthorne den Prize, he realised its mediocrity and insipid response and therefore discontinued writing books with the English setting. Naipaul recaptured his material from the postcolonial Trinidad as the prominent theme. The '*Mimic Men*' (1967) projects Trinidad as an imitative country and the people living there only as mimic men. However, Naipaul retains his familiar themes of displaced and deracinated people in the wilderness of the cross-cultural purposes and man's need to find himself in relation to the postcolonial situation there. *'A Flag on the Island'* (1967) gives a view of the political changes in Trinidad since 1940. *'The Loss of El Dorado'* (1969) examines the early history of Trinidad and gives an account of such wider events as the Europeans' search for gold and the effects of American revolutions. At this juncture of his career Naipaul felt that, having made contribution to the national awareness, he could now settle down in Trinidad. He sold h's house in London but soon got disillusioned again with Trinidad and returned to England once for all.

In the third phase England became Naipaul's steady home since any search outside England was rejected by him and he came to terms with his exiled status for ever. He overcame his earlier restlessness and took new stride as a writer of the world without any futile search for roots. Now he started taking frequent traveling to distant countries as meaningful resorts for sustaining his creative imagination which went on enriching with this widening of his horizon.

'In a Free State' (1971) which won him the Man Booker Prize, blended the autobiography and fiction. Techniquewise, it is a postmodern experiment in which he looks at 'freedom' through a cluster of stories, a novella and an excerpt from a travel diary. The meaning of freedom and the paradoxical situation in a decolonized world is the theme of this book. *'The Overcrowded Baracoon'* (1972) is a collection of articles giving disillusioned analyses of the smaller colonies.He continues the exploration of such a theme in *'Guerrillas'* (1975) which is based on the Black Power demonstrations in 1970s and the guerilla movement in Trinidad. *'A Bend in the River'* (1979) and *'The Return of Eva Paron With the Killings in Trinidad'* (1980) pick up the conflict between freedom fighters and forces in the ex-colonial countries in the aftermath of independence. Here again Naipaul's world is one of the homeless nomadic migrants making a middle passage from Africa or West Indies to England and coming back again,

for even after three hundred years, there is no system of values and not any authentic identity and things have gone out of gear in the chaos of their world in which they strive to take roots. The characters come from the rootless and half-made societies of the Third World countries and on the bend of a river—somewhere in Africa all are desperate to seize upon something to survive in the anarchy and chaos of the post—colonial period. Now Naipaul sheds has earlier joie de vivre and begins to assume the persona of a postcolonial Conrad, coolly and perceptivity examining and exposing the mutual corruption of the colonizers as well as the colonised. Even William Dalrymple who is a furious critic of most of Naipaul's works and shuns them as an interior journey, an ego-trip into himself, appreciates his craftsmanship at this stage in such words:

> "He would expose them with their own wounds and their confused and contradictory thoughts before pinning them to the page with the cool detachment of a Victorian butterfly collector. Even when one strongly disagreed with his views on politics – such as his relentless negative assessment of life in the Islamic world, or his positive spin on Hinduism and tacit support for the destruction of the Babri Maszid—it was impossible to deny the power of his writing."[8]

Here Naipaul is at his best; the detached outsider struggling to understand, taking time to go to even the most remote places and talking to people to chip away at them and their illusions. Champa Rao Mohan writes in this connection as :

> "The major themes that emerge from a reading of his novels are related to the problems of the colonized people; their sense of alienation from the landscape, their identity crisis, the paradox of freedom and the problem of neocolonialism in the ex-colonies."[9]

After his second visit to India, Naipaul wrote another

travel book *'India: A Wounded Civilization'* (1977) which picturises his disillusionment with the Indian cultural tradition as well as the pseudo self-applause and egocentric glorification by the Indian people. *'Among the Believers'* (1980) based on his travel to Pakistan and non-Arab Muslim countries, narrates his understanding and misunderstanding of Islam.

The fourth phase in Naipaul's career is marked by a series of books which blend literary genre and are also highly autobiographical. From the mid 1980s he grew older and sagacious and became mature with his own interpretation and attitude towards the world at large. He became, in his own words, a serious traveler and there has never been a vintage point for him. The world for him now became a cheerless, violent and unforgiving place. *Finding the Centre* (1984), *'The Enigma of Arrival'* (1987) and *'A Turn in the South'* (1989) belong to this phase of his writings. For the first time he examined the South America and wrote about it and it resembles the Trinidad history. As an observerand interpreter of the ex-colonies, Naipaul becomes unsparingly critical and exposes the inadequacies of such societies which he believes, to be the outcome of the unconscious acceptance of the norms and values of the colonising forces. *'The Enigma of Arrival'* is a travelogue that picturises the ordeal and evolution of Naipaul the writer on a self journey along with the realization of the futility of nostalgia. *'India : A Million Mutinies Now'* (1990) projects a new perspective from which he views India as it is a travel book about India, though different from his earlier books. *'A Way in the World'* (1994) is Naipaul's next novel on the familiar theme reiterating the expatriates' search for an authentic identity in the New World. With the publication of this book Naipaul complained of fatigue but he continued writing rather more powerful books which simultaneously attracted great appreciation and also severe criticism from the people all over the world. One of his important contributions is his address *'Our Universal Civilization'* at Manhattan, New York in 1991. It is not in a book from; nonetheless, it is an important work of Naipaul.

Naipaul's final phase of creativity begins with the turning of the 21st century since by this time he has acquired an international status and has become a legendry figure with a decolonised profile in the fast growing globalization on this earth. After famously declaring a few years ego, the sad demise of the much exhausted novel and also after labeling India as a darkness having no autonomous intellectual life, Naipaul has again made a remarkable come back and strangely enough with India on his mind. This return and aptitude is obvious in his works *'Half a Life'* (2001) followed by its extension in *'Magic Seeds'* (2004). Here, he has again used India as a fictional material but he seems to overcome his demonstrably wrong and angry indictment in *'An Area of Darkness'*. As Naipaul's view about culture is progressive, he seems to traverse his old notions with the change of time. India that was once a great hurt and from whose poverty his forefathers had to run away could not be erased by Naipaul from his mind. He seems to overcome his disillusionment as he has gone past his angry indictment in earlier works about India. 'As *The Enigma of Arrival'* picturises Naipaul's own conflict, evolution and growth as a writer, *Half a Life* must be judged as coming of age and ultimate wisdom to Naipaul and to the heroes in his fiction because, as per his own words, his works have a strong thread of continuity. It is interesting to note that such a realisation for the land of his origin happened quite late and led this prolific dissenter to accept the truth. It was really surprising when he told *'India Today'* on the eve of the publication of *'Magic Seeds'* in 2004 as: **' I can't reject India. It's going too fast, even beyond me. I'm sitting back and feeling quite happy actually.'**[10] This statement shows a cyclic progress in the sensibility of V.S. Naipaul and at this juncture he, again, realises the meaningfulness of roots in human life even if one has, like himself, learnt to grow without them.

Hence, there should remain no doubt that Naipaul's themes revolve around the growth of the writer as well as the anguish and pain of Diaspora. His new travelogues and fiction depict Naipaul's attempt to understand his own past, to come to terms with it and, to some extent, at least to silence and mitigate his nagging awareness of not being too close to India but also not too far from it. No doubt, Naipaul's intellectual bent is towards western habits as he has lived all his writing career in England, yet his works mirror the problems of the Third World people, especially the expatriates and in this last phase of his life India has again occupied his mind. So his vision has widened to be called of a cosmopolitan and to acknowledge the completion of his world view. He himself says: "**All my life I have had to think about ways of looking and how they alter the configuration of the world.**"[11] What makes him the towering figure in this movement of decolonisation and globalization is his matchlessly rich and ever progressive vision and sensibility on the one hand and an unfailing commitment to truthfulness on the other. Therefore, those high sounding critics who attribute him with the nomenclature of a *'Colonial Anglophile'* and also an a apologist for Colonialism' just on the basis of the severe indictment of the postcolonial societies in the Third World, must rectify themselves and realise the truth that he is equally sharp and severe in criticising the treacherous ways and ethnic notions of superiority in the powerful group of colonisers. For instance, Naipaul makes clear that political independence could change nothing and the imperialist powers continue to retain their hold on the former colonies through the newer and more camouflaged methods of neocolonialism. So we must acknowledge that though he is severe and unforgiving to the idiosyncratic behaviour, mimicry and foolishness of the colonised people, he never sneers at these people with any intention to please his western readers or to the fanatic Naipaulites all over the world.

Naipaul is, therefore, a novelist with diversity of assertions and enormity of controversy because by his wry assessment of the post colonial societies he has always been arousing contrasting responses. On the one hand, there are critics who pay him endless praise, while on the other, there are those who, striking the opposite chord, attack him for the unfavorable and provoking portrayal of the Third World nations both in his fiction and non-fiction. The latter are mostly scholars from the Third World particularly India, while the former are mostly from the Metropolitan western world. Much of anti-Naipaul criticism comes from West Indies and India, the two countries of his ancestry and family background. So, it will be quite useful to have a brief overview of the critical assessments and observations about V.S. Naipaul and his works.

With the idea of a separate Commonwealth literature gaining ground in the 1960s, the writers belonging to the ex-colonial English speaking world came into limelight. It was under the aegis of the Commonwealth Literature that critical studies on Naipaul first gained ascendancy and contributors poured in from various quarters. Paul Theroux, William Walsh Landeg White, Anthony Boxill, Peter Hughes and the freelance writer William Dalrymple are some of the prominent names among the western scholars on Naipaul and his literature. Some equally prominent names among the Third World critics are the West Indian scholars like George Lamming and Selwyn cudjoe and Indian critics like C.D. Narsimhaiaha, K.I. Madhusudan Rao, Sudha Rai, S. Prassanarajan and so many others. These critics mainly concentrate on Naipaul's development as a controversial writer and on the close relation between his fictional and non-fictional works and also on some of the objectionable issues relating to the portrayal of the Third World. For example, Paul Theroux is mainly interested in major themes and ideas that repeatedly occur in Naipaul's works; William Walsh highlights the extent and variety of Naipaul's artistic vision; Landeg White has focused on the ways in which Naipaul's whole career is centered on the uncertainties of his own position and has also analysed the cultural ambiguities of Naipaul's background as the pivot of all his creative endeavours. Peter Hughes's study concentrates on Naipaul's prose and shows that Naipaul's non-fiction has a deep and tangled relationship with his fiction.

George Lamming's attack on Naipaul in his book entitled '*The Pleasures of Exile*' (1960)[12] is only too well known. The other West Indian critic Selwyn Cudjoe is equally acerbic in his attack on this provocateur. In his book *V.S. Naipaul : A Materialist Reading* (1988)[13] he has tried to show that Naipaul is not politically neutral but writes from the ideological position of the west. Coming to the Indian critic, C.D. Narsimhaiaha, the renowned scholar in Commonwealth Literature and the editor of the collections on Naipaul, is less accommodating in his attitude towards this dissenter whereas K.I. Madhusudan Rao and Sudha Rai adopt a defensive stance towards the author. In his article '*V.S. Naipaul : A Split Sensibility*[14] Narsimhaiah attacks Naipaul for this lack of sympathy and concern for his own ethnic group of people in '*An Area of Darkness*'. Madhusudan Rao, in his book '*Contrary Awareness : A Critical Study of the Novels of V.S. Naipaul*' (1982)[15] closely analyses Naipaul's works and arrives at a positive conclusion that Naipaul's stance is not that of a snob who is completely bereft of all human sympathy but of a writer who, through a contrary awareness, exposes the deficiencies of the ex-colonial societies in a dispassionate manner. Sudha Rai's study '*V.S. Naipaul: A Study in Expatriate Sensibility*' (1982)[16] focuses on Naipaul's non-fiction and attempts to assess the merits of Naipaul's judgement on India. She argues that due to a complex and confusing amalgam of the Hindu-Self and the Western-Self Naipaul applies the dual cultural norms in his works and the same duality reflects in his personae. As a result he measures India by Hindu norms of *Karma, Dharma* and *Moksha* as well as the western norms of individuality and freedom.

No doubt, Naipaul maintains an unassailable distance from the land of his ancestors and speaks with a high self-esteem and uncompromising authority. Of the locations presented in his novels, while India, West Indian and Africa remain distant, inexact and sometimes even vague, London is presented with a marked exactitude and clarity. Moreover, Naipaul speaks in that trademark upper class English stutter and for him England is situated at a different level of reality—stable and at the center of Europe—while other regions can be relegated to haziness. Though living mainly in London, Naipaul has traveled frequently in the West Indies, North and South America, India and Africa. As Naipaul found every country he traveled to be a nightmare for the uprooted peoples like himself, his oeuvre expatiates this predicament of rootless ness, dereliction and non-entity of the people amidst the chaotic odds of alien lands. A close exploration of Naipaul's own soul and psyche, as visible in the works of this uprooted writer, is a necessary pursuit to make a righteous appraisal or criticism of his treatment of the theme of the immigrants stranded in foreign land and confronting with alien cultures. In his works at least three generations of Diaspora are picturised as still trying to find their feet across the seven seas. The author has displayed a distaste not only for the traditional Hindu ways of life but also for the indenture of Indians marooned in the Tropical Caribbean island with no hope of ever going back to their ancestral roots. This revulsion is indirectly expressed by the symbolic device of presenting the protagonists of his novels with a colonial rage against both the colonised as well as the colonisers.

Naipaul, though maintains his towering stature of a relentless dissenter, yet more than often he seems to be behaving like a pampered child of the western ideology. In present time, this otherwise literary giant, has become more intolerable not because of his English sensibility but because of his Narcissism and too offensive indictments to be accepted. His deliberate choice to remain non-committed or even away from the Indian or West Indian identity ishis own prerogative but the severe criticism of Gandhi, Vinoba, N.C. Chaudhary and Nehru is an unpardonable egotistical exposition of his aversion to the land of saints and of his own ancestors also. William Dalrymple is quite right in rejecting Naipaul's ego indulgence in his prerogative book *'A writer's People : Ways of Seeing and Feeling'* (2007) where this great writer has criticised and made a mockery of these great sculptures of

India. No doubt Naipaul has been a penetrating critic of life and literature, but here his nature seems to be sick with contempt for everything and everyone coming from the down-rated colonial world. Stressing on this adopted Englishness of Naipaul and his high proclaimed enmity with Indian and Indians, S. Prassanarajan comments: **"Naipaul was the one who went away, the chronicler of colonial imperfections, who entered into a Faustian deal with the colonisers."**[17]

Mahatma Gandhi was a legendry saint and thinker beyond any dispute and Gandhian philosophy and Nehru's vision are the universally accepted truths of life on earth and no spiky provocation can ever falsify these ideologies. So, whatever the glory of Naipaul the writer, he remains an affected and Narcissistic person possessing the prides and prejudices of a spoiled intellectual of modern times. That is why reviewing this author's controversial but high sounding book *'A Writer's People'* William Dalrymple has pronounced Naipaul dead as a writer. He professes, as once Brutus had done for Ceaser, to be saddened by the necessity of the assassination of Naipaul the writer since there is a tragedy here as Naipaul attempts to sacrifice even Gandhi and our cultural spiritualism perhaps only to scale greater heights as a writer of denunciations. My notion about this spoiled and perverse literary giant with magical power of language and arguments, got further strength when once again, the controversy flared up very high last year on the publication of Naipaul's biography by Petrick French under the title *'The World is what it is'*; (2007) This work publishes Naipaul's own confessions and diary records which compel us to consider him as a man with a lot of scars and blots on his character. This book reveals that Naipaul's first wife Patricia died due to depression because of his frequent visits to prostitutes. Moreover, many other women were also openly engaged with him and his English wife died due to this inhuman treatment and neglect on his part. If such a man criticises Gandhi, he deserves nothing less than condemnation and assassination.

Otherwise Naipaul has developed quite magnificently as a writer of magical power and his latest book *'A Writer's People'* (2008) is both personally moving and critically acute and invents a way of looking at a chosen section of the world through the writers he knew and also those whom he has read a new. The one thing that hasn't changed is the antipathy of Indians and pretend Indians towards his clear judgment and harsh truthfulness but he doesn't mince his words. Farrukh Dhondy writers in this regard:

> "Naipaul is unaffected by the totem and taboos that surround the subject of race and associated literary success. His way of seeing and judging is at once naive, uniformed by political correctness and objectively distance."[18]

This truth could further be justified by his assessment when he talks about a ransacked past and civilizational vandalism of India through Islamic invasions. It was the same Naipaul who was caricatured as a closet Hindu nationalist when he saw the stirrings of a nationalist revival in Indian politics. In the wake of the Gujarat riots Salman Rushdie, provoked by Naipaul's earlier anti-Muslim pronouncements, called him **'a fellow traveller of Fascism who has disgraced the Nobel.'**[19] Moreover, there was an irony in the timing : the Nobel was announced in October 2001, in the after roar of 9/11 attacks. Naipaul, much to the displeasure of both the left as well as the right establishments, has been talking about Islam and its fundamental agenda. *'Among the Believers : An Islamic Journey'* (1981) and its sequel *'Beyond Belief : Islamic Excursions Among the Converted Peoples'* (1998) both have born out of his travels in Iran, Pakistan, Malaysia and Indonesia and bring out in ruthless precision how Islam as a religion of conversion destroys the past. He opines: **"Islam in its origin is an Arab religion. Everyone not an Arab who is a Muslim is a convert. Islam is not simply a matter of coincidence or private belief. It makes imperial demands."**[20]

Naipaul further states that the story of Pakistan is a terror story. All these deliberations have enraged the fanatic Muslims but in these prophetic observations, Naipaul could foresee the wreckage looming at large. Much before the radical Islamic terrorism came to dominate the glossary of the past 9/11 world, Naipaul, who otherwise is politically incorrect, was speaking this unpleasant truth to the western world of cosy illusions. It is equally true that the empire might have shaped his life as a writer, Naipaul is not less brutal in his rejoinder to the welfare state that has been eating away the British civilization as revealed in *'Magic Seeds'*.

Thus, in spite of residing in England, Naipaul has emerged as a decolonised cosmopolitan and in his delineation of the colonised as well as colonizers he is not even a little bothered about his fame or criticism at all. Moreover, unlike the new generation of postcolonial writers, Naipaul's lack of roots is a burden that he carries with him during his restless travels around the world but it is also his weapon with which he could ironically slice up the countries he visits. It is actually the source of his strength as well as his acerbity. However, his enrichment through cross—cultural experiences places him at a position that shapes his sensibility to render a detached account of this world. This surgeon-like objectivity and non-attachment of Naipaul becomes a prerogative and he does not spare anyone irrespective of race, class or nationality and herein lies the secret of his universal popularity. Above all, the world is still too much of whirls and upheavals to keep Naipaul as a retired writer or as a prophet at rest in his private hermitage in the English countryside of Wiltshire. So, there is no doubt that he is a giant writer with extraordinary vision and sensibility that have come to him through a long exposure to struggle, migration, memory and the pure wonderment of looking while seeing and listening while hearing across the world. It is equally noteworthy that it is the personal nature of the anguish experienced by Naipaul himself that defines his vision and sets the tone of his works. When in 2001 the Swedish

Academy finally gave the Nobel Prize to him "**for having united perceptive narrative and incorruptible scrutiny in works that compel us to see the presence of suppressed histories,**"[21] the hardcore Naipaulites thought it was a belated recognition.

References

1. V.S. Naipaul, *'The Return of Eva Peron with the Killings in Trinidad,* (Harmondsworth: Penguin Books,*1981),* p. 21.
2. Elbaki Hermassi, *The Third World Reassessed,* (Berkeley: University of California Press, 1980), p. 167.
3. See quoted in S. Prassanarajan, 'V S. Naipaul: The Provocateur' *'India Today'*. (New Delhi : 10 Sept. 2007), p. 56.
4. V.S. Naipaul, *The Overcrowded Barracoon,* (London: Penguin Books, Reprint 1984), pp. 32-50.
5. Bibu Padhi, *Naipaul on Naipaul and The Novel;* Modern Fiction Studies, p. 458.
6. V.S. Naipaul, *The Overcrowded Barracoon,* op. cit., p. 28.
7. Idem.
8. William Dalrymple, 'An Aria of Darkness : Naipaul's New Book Traverses Old Ground; *Outlook,* (New Delhi: 24 Sept. 2007), p. 80.
9. Champa Rao Mohan, *Postcolonial Situation in the Novels of V.S. Naipaul,*(New Delhi : Atlantic Publishers & Distributors, 2004), p. 8.
10. S. Prassanarajan, 'V.S. Naipaul : The Provocateur'; *India Today,* op. cit., p. 54.
11. V.S. Naipaul, Returning to the Centre; *The Sunday Express* (New Delhi: 06, Sept. 2007), p. 3.
12. George Lamming, *The Pleasures of Exile* (London: Michael Joseph, 1960).
13. Selvyn Cudjoe, *V.S. Naipaul: A Materialist Reading* (Amherst: University of Massachusettes Press, 1988).
14. C.D. Narsimhaiah, *The Critical Indian Scene: Controversial Essays* (Delhi : B.R. Publishing Crop. 1990) p. 96–109.

15. K.I. Madhusudan Rao, *Contrary Awareness: A Critical Study of the Novels of V.S. Naipaul* (Guntur: Saradhi, 1982).
16. Sudha Rai, *V.S. Naipaul: A Study in Expatriate Sensibility*, (New Delhi: Arnold Heinmann, 1982).
17. S. Prassanarajan, *India Today*, op. cit., p. 56.
18. Farrukh Dhondy, All Unrepentant Writers: *The Times of India* (New Delhi: 24 Sept. 2007), p. 12.
19. Salman Rushdie; see quoted in S. Prassanarajan's *V.S. Naipaul:* The Provocateur. *India Today*, (New Delhi : 10, Sept. 2007), p. 56.
20. V.S. Naipaul; see quoted in S. Prassanarajan, op. cit., p. 560.
21. Idem.

3

Cultural Disintegration and Immigrants' Quest for Identity in Limbo

> *"This (modern) colonialism colonizes minds in addition to bodies and it releases forces within the colonized societies to alter their cultural priorities once for all. In the process in helps generalise the concept of the modern West from a geographical and temporal entity to a psychological category. The West is now everywhere, within the West and outside, in structures and in minds."*[1]
>
> *– Ashis Nandy*

V.S. Naipaul, being a Trinidad born Indian, articulates the predicament of East Indian immigrants who are uprooted and have gradually lost their Indianness due to a long exposure to the influences of the Creole culture as well as to the cultural colonization under the imperial powers. In his early novels that form the Trinidad tetralogy – *'The Mystic Masseur' (1957), 'The Suffrage of Elvira' (1958). 'Miguel Street'* (1959) and *'A House of Mr. Biswas'* (1961) Naipaul deals predominantly with the East Indians' experiences in the West

Indies. These novels present a poignant picture of their struggle to preserve their past identity in alien environment; the inevitable disintegration and loss of their selfhood with no hope of some substitute identity any more. *'The Mystic Masseur'* is set in Port of Spain and the rural areas of Trinidad amidst Indians. The narrator speaks its theme as **"the history of Ganesh is, in a way the history of our times.**"[2] It is a comic study of the postcolonial political rise and expatriate Indians' response which smacks of mutual self-deception. Ganesh, the hero of the novel, is a representative figure of East Indians in Trinidad in their move towards city life and their subsequent Creolization. The novel is an allegory of the history of the Hindu community and Ganesh represents the first generation of the East Indians to come under the influence of the western education which acted as a potent force for cultural colonisation. It is the need for education that brings Ganesh to the Creole world where there is a different value system. Mr. Ramsumair, Ganesh's father, makes special preparations for the day Ganesh, in spite of all his awkwardness, is to be enrolled in Queen's Royal College:

> "Mr. Ramsumair made a lot of noise about sending his son to the 'town college' and the week before the term began he took Ganesh all over the district, showing him off to friends and acquaintances. He had Ganesh dressed in a Khaki suit and a Khaki Toupee and many people said the boy looked like a little sahib."[3]

The novel centers around the meteoric rise and metamorphosis of Ganesh, the protagonist, who represents the East Indians under the process of acculturisation. Ganesh feels awkward and experiences a humiliation when the boys make a fun of his dress and country manners. This awkwardness comes to him, as the narrator points out, more because of his Indian name. He comes to realise the marginalised position of Indians and even tries to hide his Indian identity: "**Ganesh never lost his awkwardness. He**

was so ashamed of his Indian name that for a while he spread a story that he was really called Gareth."[4]

Through Ganesh's character the narrator is expressing his views about the contemporary Trinidadian Hindus whose ancestors had indentured here from India and who lived a very circumscribed life as laborers. Set in the West Indies on the eve of its independence, this novel highlights displaced and mediocre East Indian individuals in pursuit of recognition and success. Ganesh is a representative of the community which, according to the author, is peasant-minded, money-minded, spiritually static but cut off from its roots and set in a materialist colonial society. The subtle process of cultural colonisation has already begun with the moment of Ganesh's contact with colonizing culture. Four years of his stay at college have influenced Ganesh quite enough to go against the traditional custom of marriage. When Ganesh refuses to accept his father's selection of a bride for him he gets a strong warning, rather an ultimatum, that if Ganesh doesn't want to get married he must consider himself an orphan. Instead of returning home Ganesh disobeys his father and gets enrolled in the Government Training College for teachers. He finally returns home only when he receives a telegram and on arriving at Fourways, he gets the news of his father's death. The short interlude between Ganesh's disagreement with his father and his return from Port of Spain is significant because it provides a glimpse of a typical colonial school. The headmaster of the school gives Ganesh a brief on the purpose of education as to form not inform.

The narrator writes about Ganesh with timely comments, juxtaposition and humorous deflation to reveal the absurdity of the society. In ironic words he observes: **"Ganesh gave up trying to teach the boys anything and was happy enough to note a week-to-week improvement in his record Book."**[5] Through the medium of the narrator within the novel Naipaul demonstrates his own technique as a novelist since he remains detached and allows the characters to damn themselves. From the point of Ganesh's return to Fourways until his final move to Port of Spain, the narrator oscillates between Fourways and Fuente Grove and traces the progress story of Ganesh upto his victory in election and his first appearance as an M.L.C. and then his rise in position to M.B.E. Thus, the narrator makes it clear that political power is ultimately an embodiment of the dream of power, possession and self-realisation for the colonised peoples. However, the narrative identifies the destiny of the country with the personality of the gradually emerging political leaders like Ganesh. Harihar Rath in his critical essay on the novel has written thus:

> "Strangely enough all the qualities of Ganesh are not really virtuous, but the only working expediency which is most indispensable and suitable for any individual to succeed in the Caribbean society during the transitional period between the disappearance of the older values and the appearance of a new cultural loyalty and standard."[6]

Ganesh's aunt, who is nicknamed as 'the Great Belcher' is a constant presence in the novel and she is the first person to convince him that he has the potentials of a mystic. Apart from this she has great organising capabilities and is continually on circuit organising funerals and marriages in her own community and we get the feels of the community life of the East Indians in Trinidad. However, we are also made aware that the inner bastions of the East Indian culture have begun to collapse. This section of the novel also focuses on the scene of cultural upheaval already set in motion by the colonial education and how it got the momentum through the modernizing forces unleashed by the Second World War. The economic boom precipitated by the American presence in Trinidad, together with rapid urbanisation, acted as potent external force boosting this disintegration. The writer articulates the predicament of stagnant society that the East Indians had managed to recreate in Trinidad. It was an India in isolation and its insulator fell away and was shattered to pieces during the Second World War. In *'The Mystic Masseur'* Naipaul relates the story of Ganesh an ascent—infatuated individual in a non-holds-barred rag-to-riches framework. Though there is nothing to fault in individual's attempt at escaping his existential obscurity and social non-entity, yet at another level of the sardonic commentary of the narrator Naipaul also brings forth the dichotomy in the lives of the East Indians in Trinidad. The biographical account of Ganesh is double–edged as it takes the lid off the Trinidadian world of chicanery, betrayal and falsehood.

The degradation in the religion of East Indians, which has been reduced merely to rites without philosophy, becomes evident during Ganesh's initiation ceremony, his practices as mystic, his marriage and his behaviour at the temple that is constructed in Fuente Grove to attract the American soldiers. When Ganesh undergoes the initiation ceremony to become a real Brahmin as per Hindu custom his head is shaved and he is given a little saffron bundle and asked to go Benaras to study. When Ganesh keeps on walking away and does not turn back his steps all are bewildered. In keeping with the custom, Dookhie bursts out in anger:

> "Cut out this nonsense, man. Stop behaving stupid. You think I have all day to run after you ? You think you really going to Benaras ? That is in India, you know, and this is Trinidad."[7]

These reactions make clear the mimicry and the limitations of the make-believe world of the East Indians who are adhering to distant traditions just for the sake of their illusionary Hinduism. The narrator's formal treatment of the history of Ganesh is really a carefully controlled piece of satiric inflation. Ganesh's manner of treating the narrator who comes to the masseur for treatment of his hot and swollen foot - his laying the body on a blanket on the floor, examining him, mumbling a Hindi couplet over his body and diagnosing the disease as nothing but bad blood—is all symptomatic of a quack whose chicanery is quite apparent. The dichotomy is further exemplified during Ganesh's marriage. In a traditional Hindu marriage, the groom is not supposed to see the bride before marriage. However, Ganesh and Leela have already met each other. So Ramlogan, Leela's father and Ganesh have to pretend that Ganesh has never seen Leela otherwise in Trinidad they shall no longer be looked as good Hindus. It is most important that he does not eat until he extracts a sizeable dowry from Ramlogan. They can only act like good Hindus because of sentimental values attached to their traditions knowing fully well that at Founte Grove he will succeed as a businessman if he increases his reputation as a spiritual healer and he leaves no stone unturned to achieve it. It is ironic that he becomes a member of the legislative assembly by virtue of his mystical character. He is clever in climaxing his political campaign by organising a seven day recitation of Bhagwat because he knows the religious leanings of his people. The duplicity of his character comes to the surface when he condemns the labour movement of the people by supporting the British colonialists. After achieving political motifs by manipulating his Indian heritage he kicks it by changing his name to G.R. Miur. Thus *'The Mystic Masseur'* illustrates Naipaul's stance on mimicry as a theme. In the words of the narrator the life of Ganesh—a quack masseur, a false mystic, a phony author and a corrupt politician—becomes an allegory of the history of the time and the novel as a whole, is an account of the apotheosis of one man who represents the whole community. It is also interesting to note that to highlight his mysticism and to deceive people he wears Indian dhoti and koorta, but he prefers to wear European dresses on other occasions. His house has a Hindu exterior but the interior has all the modern European scientific gadgets. Thus, hero in politics is also its villain. Hariher Rath and K.C. Mishra have also commented in their article *'The Mystic Masseur: A study in Third-World Politics'* as :

> "It is also seen that Naipaul is adopting similar technique of incorporating images and symbols to highlight Ganesh's imitation and fraudulence. His portrayal gives us an impression that even though

> he is victimised, he rises to be the master of all confusion."[8]

The cultural disintegration is wide spread among the East Indians and even his political rivals also anglicise their names as Beharry and Cryus Stephen Narayan for similar acceptance.

The theme of political decadence has been intensified by the choice of images and symbols. The setting of the novel, thus, emphasises the way Trinidadians have been alienated from their surroundings, suggesting that their identities have been disintegrated. The East Indians themselves are unable to see the contradiction because the process of cultural colonisation has worked on them unconsciously. It is this aspect of the society of Trinidad that Naipaul has tried to capture in the novel. Champa Rao Mohan also agrees with this opinion when she writes:

> "Naipaul draws attentions to the inadequacies of colonial societies which are often characterised by a lack of acumen for specialization. Trinidad is portrayed as a society in upheaval, where the old order is giving way to new forces of modernity and the East Indian community of which Ganesh is a representative is particularly vulnerable. Ganesh's success story is really the story of the disintegration of the East Indian community, which under the conflicting pull of the Eastern and Western world, makes the final choice in favour of the Western civilization."[9]

Naipaul's next novel *'The Suffrage of Elvira'* (1958) was written to picturise the political dimensions of Trinidadian society in the era of the post-colonial upheaval. While *'The Mystic Masseur'* focuses on the rural society of the East Indians, this novel completes the picture by examining the society where democracy is a new born baby crying and struggling to grow. *'The Suffrage of Elvira'* is constructed around a single event of the second general elections in Elvira. During this period of growing social and political awareness after the upheaval, the East Indian community experiences the new emerging concepts of democracy. This novel picks up the strands of the story at the point where *'The Mystic Masseur'* had left off. It opens up into the broader social context of multiracial Elvira and includes the Negro and Spanish population as well. Moreover, there are definite references in it to the characters and events which make it clear that the novel is a continuation of the previous one. For example, in chapter six there is a specific reference to Ganesh. After Herbert's spiritual fumigation Baksh says: "**Ganesh Pundit was really the man for this sort of mystic things. Pity he had to take politics. Still that show-how good he was. The moment he feel he was losing his hand for that sort of thing, he give up the business.**"[10]

Ramlogan also reappears here as the owner of a Rumshop and his identity as the same Ramlogan is confirmed from what Chittranjan says about him in the second chapter: "**For three years now, since the man come to live in Elvira, he only giving me provocation**"[11] A reference to the first general elections of nineteen forty-six, the major event in the preceding novels, also reiterates the continuation of the thematic current of the story. This novel demonstrates how unsuitable the modern concept of democracy is for a corrupt and divided colonial society in which democracy loses all meanings and becomes a means for promoting self-interests. Actually, universal adult suffrage came to Trinidad in nineteen forty-six taking the people with surprise. By the second general elections, however, people had become aware of the values of their votes and were out to exploit the candidates. When Harbans, the Hindu candidate, tells Baksh, the Muslim vote bank that in nineteen forty six none of the candidates he knew had spent as much as he was having to, Baksh immediately replies. "**But that was only the first election. People did just go and vote for the man they like. Now is different. People learning. You have to spend on them.**"[12]

Under the new circumstances only the Philistine values dominate and determine which candidate would win the elections. The disintegration of the East Indians is apparent in their opportunism and selfishness. Everyone is out to take bribes and Indians do not bother about their Hindu candidates since for them money and selfishness is above any other consideration. Harichand, the printer, blackmails, Harbans: **"If you want my vote, you want my printer."**[13]. Naipaul reveals the truth that no one owes any loyalty to the island and scarcely any to his group since both the candidates as well as the electorates are tricksters. Harbans is prepared to give any bribe for votes and therefore concedes to Baksh's demands though it far exceeds what was initially agreed upon. He even goes to the extent of trading a marriage alliance with Chittaranjan who bargains the marriage of his daughter Nelly to Harban's son. Money is placed topmost, even above religion and traditional values have become a farce now. Under the influence of capitalism people have turned into worshippers of Mammon. This is evident in the second chapter when the reason for Chittaranjan's importance is expressed: **"Easily the most important person in Elvira was Chittaranjan. And there was no mystery why. He looked rich and was rich."**[14]

The overwhelming influence of materialism and the Elvirans' propensity for money is revealed in their priorities and opportunism for the sake of money. Baksh, the other power of Elvira, becomes the Muslim leader because he is a man of reputed wealth, even though he is not a good Muslim:

> "It was puzzle: how Baksh came to be the Muslim leader. He wans't a good Muslim. He didn't know all the injunction of the Prophet and those he did know he broke. For instance he was a great drinker."[15]

Everyone is out to play the foul game and there is total disintegration all around. There is an utter confusion just before the elections with everyone selling out to somebody. It is Harbans who wins the election by adopting all means fair and foul and so it leaves a very bitter taste in his mouth.

His brand new jaguar is set on fire in the final scene when Harbans comes to Elvira for the first time after becoming a Member of Legislative Council to give away the case of whisky which Romlogan had promised the committee of the winning candidate. Yet Harbans himself is in a way responsible for what happens as the passage shows:

> "He wasn't the candidate they knew. Gone was the informality of dress, the loose trousers, the tie around the waist, the open shirt. He was in a double-breasted grey suit.... Harbans didn't wave. He looked preoccupied, kept his eye on the ground, and when he hawked and spat in the gutter, pulled out an ironed handkerchief and wiped his lips—not wiped even, patted them—in fussiest way."[16]

Harbans's degradation into a typical politician is complete at the end of the novel when he goes back on his promise to Chittaranjan on the pretext of the false scandal involving Nelly and Foam. When Chittaranjan visits Harbans in Port of Spain, the latter acts busy, remains tight-lipped and cool. The cultural confusion and the breakdown of traditional values and religiosity are aptly described in the novel. The acculturation of the rootless East Indians is a major theme in these early novels of Naipaul and though this novel revolves around a political event, it exposes the social tensions and bickering of a heterogeneous society like Trinidad. All this is exposed in the passages like the following:

> "Things were crazily mixed up in Elvira. Everybody, Hindus, Muslims and Christians, owned a Bible; the Hindus and Muslims looking on it, if anything, with greater awe. Hindus and Muslims celebrated Christmas and Easter. The Spaniards and some of the Negroes celebrated the Hindu festival of lights. Someone had told them that Lakshmi, the Goodess of prosperity, was being honored; they placed small earthen lamps on their money-boxes and waited, as they said, for the money to breed. Everybody

> celebrated the Muslim festival of Hosein. In fact, when Elvira was done with religious festivals, there were few straight days left."[17]

The novel is superb in its exposition of that mechanism of the functioning of the democratic process and its initial filtering down to the common people. The machinery of election is educative and brings out not only the dormant differences but also a temporarily forged unity created by a common involvement in the election. But this impression of amity is nothing more than a confusing illusion and all the feelings of religious and racial hatred flare up when election brings all these prejudices to surface. The false scandal involving Nelly and Foam exposes the racial relation in Elvira and Chittaranjan and Baksh are naked in their hostility. **"What is Muslim"**[18] Baksh's retort is equally venomous : "**All you is just a pack of Kaffir, if you ask me**"[19].

While portraying the socio-cultural degradation of the East Indians, Naipaul provides us a close view of the society in turmoil. The cultural confusion of the East Indians is also clearly evident in their dresses which are more pronouncedly western. Mrs. Baksh wears skirts instead of the traditional Muslim attire. Even Pundit Dhaniram, the best known pundit in Elvira, wears a dhoti only occasionally and prefers to wear Khaki trousers, yellow sports shirt, brown felt hat and brown patent leather shoes. Pundit Dhaniram is educated at a Presbyterian school and sings hymns and his training in the Christian school is a matter of pride for him because it makes him see both sides. The East Indians of multi-racial Elvira are also as out of touch with Hindi as the East Indians portrayed in Masseur. Except for Dhaniram's invalid wife, no one else speaks their ancestral language.

It is equally noteworthy that traditions have also yielded to the powerful whirl of modernity and so conventional customs should also yield to political interests. In the grip of materialistic considerations things have turned upside down. For instance, while in a conventional Hindu marriage it is the girl's father who is expected to humbly approach the boy's father for an alliance but in this novel, we notice quite an opposite happening. Harbans wants the votes controlled by Chittranjan and so it is he who has to be solicitous. The breakdown of the Hindu social order is also suggested through incidents like Dhaniram's daughter-in-law's elopement with Lorkhoor. The influence of the new socio-political trends is quite evident on the behaviour patterns of the people.

What makes *'The Suffrage of Elvira'* different from the other novels in the grouping is the inclusion of Negro characters. There are four in all : Preacher, Cuffy, Sebastian, and Teacher Francis. Naipaul's handling of these characters lacks the depth he shows in the delineation of the East Indian characters. Preacher's role as one of the candidates is substantial one, but his characterisation borders on the grotesque. Sebastian is just a minor character who hardly speaks, but his presence lends a comic touch to the novel. Mr. Cuffy, in spite of being a more substantial character compared to Preacher and Sebastian, somehow appears insipid. He is dull as a living character but his death, over which a lot of fuss is made by Harbans and his party members for the sake of publicity, creates a sensation. The most convincing of all the Negro characters in the novel is Teacher Francis, and though he plays no major role, yet is more accessible to us. He views the events with an intelligent detachment and provides wise comments about the elections. Naipaul however disposes off this character quite suddenly halfway and we come to know at the end that he deteriorated rapidly in Port of Spain. The novelist, on the whole, seems uncomfortable in handling the Negro characters and does not display the same dexterity as he does in the portrayal of the East Indians. It is perhaps because Naipaul's early childhood upbringing was in the enclosed Indian community with hardly a contact with the Negro world since the two communities in Trinidad were juxtaposed and mutually exclusive.

This novel has simultaneously received all commendation

as well as bitter condemnation from the critics and their arguments are overwhelming to the readers. Landeg White appreciates the novel for its tightly knit story but also points out that this has been achieved by restoring to "**a good deal of caricature.**"[20] The idea he seeks to put across is that though noble human qualities are as much present in Trinidad as anywhere else, they cannot flower in the stultifying colonial environment of Trinidad. Initially Naipaul did not find a favourable response in the electoral circles of the West Indies. George Lamming, a fellow West Indian novelist, who came out with a bitter criticism while assessing these early novels of Naipaul, has observed as:

> "His books can't move beyond a castrated satire; and although satire may be a useful element in fiction, no important work, comparable to Selvon's can rest safely on satire alone. When such a writer is a colonial, ashamed of his cultural background and striving like mad to prove himself through promotion to the peaks of a 'superior' culture whose values are gravely in doubt, then satire, like the charge of philistinism, is for me nothing more than a refuge. And it is too small a refuge for a writer who wishes to be taken seriously."[21]

This attack appears to be motivated by personal reasons, but there is certainly an element of truth in it so far as the ending of the novel is concerned. While for the most part his irony is tinged with good humour and understanding there are moments when his satire assumes sharpness. One such instance is evident towards the end of this novel when Harban's car is set on fire and he cries out in disgust and hatred: "**Elvira, you is a bitch.**"[22] and leaves Elvira. It is perhaps, the note of rejection on which the novel ends that is unacceptable to Lamming who believes that novels which expose the inadequacies of underprivileged societies like the West Indies, should employ a sympathetic approach. But Naipaul is not an irresponsible ironist as some critics think. On the contrary, it is his commitment to truth as well as his belief in the novel as a form of social enquiry that makes him reveal the shortcomings of his society as well as other colonial societies. Even in *'The Suffrage of Elvira'* there is a constant awareness of the slave part of the West Indies; it forms only one of the many strands that inform his larger vision.

Naipaul's next novel is *'Miguel Street'*, although first to be composed in 1955, yet published in 1959 and therefore comes third in the chronological order. This analysis would consider *'Miguel Street'* in the order of its publication so as to maintain the overall sense of continuity in theme and setting of Naipaul's novels. For while *'The Suffrage of Elvira'* focuses on its multiracial aspect, it is logically correct that *'Miguel Street'* should be set in Port of Spain and add the third dimension to the picture of Trinidad. So far as the theme of cultural disintegration of the East Indian community is concerned, it demonstrates the marginal position of the East Indians in the Creole dominated Port of Spain. In this novel Naipaul deals comically but equally sensitively with The East Indians' struggle to find a foothold in the fluidity and flux of the new world. Deeply involved in the colonized people's quest for order and identity, Naipaul makes these aspects central to this novel also. Yashoda Bhat writes in this regard: "**Miguel Street is comedy based on the amused revelation of the inconsistencies and follies of the Trinidad world of commons. Underlying the comedy, however there is also an exploration of the basic motives behind human action**"[23]. The East Indians form a small minority in the *'Miguel Street'*. Bhaku's is the only other Indian family living in the street apart from the narrator and his mother. Then there is Bogart who happens to be a real-life character as Naipaul himself has said. Bibhu Padi writes of this character : "**By bringing the lovely, real-life character of Bogart into his fiction Naipaul was restating the aimlessness, the rootless isolation of the Indians in the West Indies.**"[24]

Bhaku, who belongs to an older generation of Indians, can sing verses from the *Ramyana*. His wife proudly claims that her husband can read and write Hindi as well as English. When the narrator's mother tells her that Bhaku should get some work her reply is: **"you could see he working with all the rude and crude people it have here in Port of Spain**."[25] It is clear that the Bhakus maintain their distance from the Creoles who form the majority in the street. The tension that exists between the two races is made implicit. The narrator, however, being of a much younger generation and having grown up in the street feels no such inhibitions. The novel consists of seventeen loosely interlinked episodes each of which focuses on one particular character inhabiting the street. It is more a series of character sketches than a novel, however, the episodes are held together by the common setting as well as the common first person narrator, through whose perspective we view the slum world of the street. The narrator, who has come to the street from Chaguanas a year or two before the war, recounts things as they appear to him as a boy living in the street. The episodes together complete the picture of a typical picaroon society, which has no set standards for anything. Drawing attention to this aspect of the society in Trinidad in *'The Middle Passage'* Naipaul observes:

> "To condemn the picaroon society out of hand is to ignore its important quality. And this is not its ability to beguile and enchant. For if such a society breeds cynicism, it also breeds tolerance, not the tolerance between castes and creeds and so on—which does not exist in Trinidad anyway—but something more profound: tolerance for every human activity and affection for every demonstration of wit and style."[26]

The residents of the Miguel street are natural eccentrics and it is through their eccentric behaviour that the characters seek to break the tedium of their lives and get noticed. The narrator sees the street as a world where everybody is quite different from everybody else. Man-man is mad; George, stupid; Big Foot, a bully; Hat, an adventurer; Popo, philosopher and Morgan, a comedian. Yet in order to become an accepted member of the street gang it is necessary to have something in common. The variety lies only in the masks of eccentricity that the residents of the street wear to get themselves noticed. This is not to say that the street is devoid of individuals with genuine yearnings. There are characters like Popo, B. Wordsworth and Elias who are not fake but their yearnings are sadly out of tune with their environment. Popo, the carpenter, is poetic man, who is always busy hammering and sawing. His wish to be creative and original is evident in his untiring efforts to give shape to the thing without a name. But when his wife elopes he is forced to become materialistic enough to steal and sell other's furniture. Elias wants to be a doctor but ends up as a scavenging cart driver. B. Wordsworth claims a spiritual kinship with the poet William Wordsworth and is fanciful and vain to become the greatest poet of nature.

Two characteristics about the social life of the Creole Negroes are especially noticeable in this novel. Their causal attitude to illegitimacy and the brutality towards women and children are the residual elements of their past life of slavery. Denied of a family life during the days of slavery, the Negroes could only form casual relationships. On the other hand, physical brutality of the strong towards the weak being the basis of the slave system, it was also resorted to by the slaves as a means of psychological release and became a common feature of West Indies life.

Most of the man-woman relationships portrayed in *'Miguel Street'* are of a casual nature. In the first story entitled "Bogart' when Bogart suddenly disappears from the street, Hat and his friend begin to use Bogart's room as their club-house. They play cards, drink and even bring the odd stray women to the room. Eddoes is caught off-guard when Bogart returns suddenly and discovers him with a woman. In the story 'George and the Pink House', when George's wife dies, he simply brings another woman and when even she leaves, he converts his house into a brothel and starts entertaining American soldiers. Hat voices the typical attitude to marriage in 'Until the Soldiers Came', when his brother Edwards says that he has to get married because his girlfriend is making baby. Hat remarks scornfully:

> "Is a damn funny thing to say. If everybody married because woman making baby for them it go to be a hell of a thing. What happen that you want to be different now from everybody else in Trinidad ? You come so American."[27]

Even among married couples loyalty is a rare thing. In 'The Thing Without a Name' Popo's wife elopes with the gardener of the big house where she works as a cook. She, however, returns to Popo after he has painted and furnished his house. The case of Mrs. Hereira in 'Love, Love, Love Alone' is somewhat different. She leaves her wealthy husband who is a doctor and goes to a man called Toni only for the sake of love but on being abused she returns to her husband to settle for comforts even without love.

In the street child beating and woman-battering is a common everyday affair. For George it is a recreational activity, entertaining enough to keep him from joining the street gang. For Bhaku, beating his wife is a ritual. He uses a cricket bat for the purpose and Mrs. Bhaku herself keeps the bat well-oiled and ready for use. In the Indian context also wife beating is accepted as the husband's prerogative. The general attitude is summed up as: **"Every now and then just knock them down, Every now and then just throw them down, Black up their eye and bruise up their knee, And then they love you eternally."**[28]

Children are treated no better in the Trinidadian society where heterogeneous admixture of races has no sense of individual dignity for a human being. When the narrator and Hat's nephews, Boyee and Errol, are together they compare notes about beating and Boyee says: **"The blow we get is nothing to what Big Foot used to get from his father."**[29] Hat supplements the information:

> "Everyday Big Foot father, the policeman, giving Big

> Foot blows. Like medicine. Three times a day after meals. And here Big Foot talk afterwards. He used to say, when I get big and have children, I go beat them, beat them."[30]

The narrator's comment provides a psychological insight as to how brutality becomes self-perpetuating: **"I didn't say it then, because I was ashamed : but I had often, felt the same way when my mother beat me."**[31]

Though there is much laughter in street, the stories demonstrate that the world is a 'stupid, sad place' and the narrator realises this through Laura, the prostitute. She is the most vivacious and gay person in the street, but when Laura's eldest daughter comes home one night and tells her – **"Ma, I going to make baby"**[32] Laura's defenses crumble and she begins to cry. The narrator's comment shows that laughter is one of the masks of bravado that each character wears to hide the bitter reality of their lives. Naipaul, even amidst the boisterous laughter, never allows us to loose sight of the central tragedy in the lives of the residents of 'Miguel Street.' It is exemplified even in the case of Dolly, George's daughter. In spite of being beaten up by her father Dolly is always giggling.

An idea that frequently rises in this novel is that the inadequacy of the colonial society requires no efficiency. To the residents of *'Miguel Street'* England and America are the only places where any thing of worth is possible. Admiration for America is the latest craze and everyone tries to emulate American mannerisms. When Bogart returns after disappearing for the second time, the narrator notices Bogart's deliberate imitation of American behaviour patterns. During the Second World War when the American soldiers flood Trinidad, Edward gets a job with them in Chaguanas and becomes a complete emulator of them. By the end of the novel, there is a complete change even in the narrator's attitude to Trinidad. When his mother rebukes him for his wild dissolute ways, he blames Trinidad for it, **"Is not my fault really. Is just Trinidad. What else everybody can do here**

except drink?"[33] It seems that the only hope lies in rejection and escape because this novel also ends on the note of rejection with the narrator's departure to London.

Naipaul's craftsmanship is evident in the expert handling of the narrative technique also. By exploiting the single first person narrator's dual perspectives, as a child and as a grown-up recalling his childhood, Naipaul is able to recreate his childhood experiences and at the same time to avoid making judgment. The ironic gap between the child's innocent views of things and the critical but detached account of the grown-up narrator recalling his childhood experiences is enough to convey the true picture of Trinidadian society and its amoral status. *'Miguel Street'* emerges as a symbol of the tragic-comic situation of man in the new world environment. As opportunity does not lend itself to ambition, the residents of street can do little more than take refuse in fantasy. In an amoral and tolerant society that lays no standards, personality can not crystallize into a meaningful entity but remains fluid and shapeless. Consequently the quests for meaning carried out within the society end in failure. The only success story of *'Miguel Street'* is the narrator's whose also is a story of escape.

'A House for Mr. Biswas' (1961) is the masterpiece of Naipaul as it presents the classic struggle of a third generation Indian for an authentic selfhood within the alien environment of Trinidad. While the preceding novels examine the social and political aspects of colonial Trinidad *'A House for Mr. Biswas'* delves deeper into the psyche of an individual to reveal the major problematic of the dispossessed individual carving for an authentic existence. The novel is epic in scope and a saga of the struggle of an individual Indian against the fluidity of colonial life under the new forces and trends which have caused a breakdown of the historical past as well as the instable present in the transplanted society of the island. The story of Mr. Biswas with all the absurdities in the aftermath of imperial chaos, exposes the wounds of East Indians who are long exiled and whose historical Indianness is nothing more than a dead burden on them. Here Naipaul

depicts the struggle of a desperate individual for an identity and selfhood in the uprooted East Indian society of Trinidad which vehemently denies it. Mr. Biswas's struggle to carve a right niche for his self in a hostile environment is trifled by communal pressures and constant suspensions of life as the socio-cultural disintegration and deracination of his society has wrought only neglect, surveillance and degradation. The novel is a tragi-comic dramatisation of the self-assertion of a man against the evils of fluid life through the detailed activities of a household of Indian origin in the second and third generation of decadent Hindu cultural legacy in the alien world. Bruce F. MacDonald points out:

> "Mr. Biswas, like Ganesh, is a Trinidad Hindu but he was born when thinking of his society had already moved towards the west and away from India. Hinduism has not completely broken down but is succumbing to the seepage from the surrounding society."[34]

Certainly the story of Mr. Biswas captures the West Indian life dialect, natural setting and upheavals but it picturises the socio-cultural erosion of East Indians. By assuming the role of an official biographer and constantly referring to the protagonist as Mr. Biswas, Naipaul achieves a kind of detachment that enables him tu present the protagonist simultaneously as absurd and heroic. According to Robert D. Hamner:

> "Through his hero's various associations and experiences with people in different places and degrees of life, Naipaul is allowed excellent opportunity to satirise the social classes. With some degrees of fantasy in a few episodes the novel is nonetheless pre-dominantly realistic (sometimes scatological) in its attention to vivid detail, its adherence to the plane of low life and its candid, straight forward presentation— — — — Mr. Biswas is identifiable with the background out of which he attempts desperately,

> despairingly to escape; he plays the fool combining realism and fantasy in comic situations which often take on the proportions of melodrama because of his overtly emotional involvement with those around him. But at the same time he possesses sensitive, intellectual qualities which, as they are handled by the author, impose his own sense of proportion on the world."[35]

This novel, in a sense, is the social history of the Indians in Trinidad and the struggle of an individual is symbolically presented as the need of every rootless man to develop an authentic selfhood in exiled status. While the cultural clash and the gradual disintegration of the Indian community still forms the major preoccupation in the novel, Naipaul at the same time focuses on the related problem of the Indians struggle for finding a foothold in the *'New World.'*

Divided into manageable sections the story of the novel moves forward progressively and each section deals with a different phase of Mr. Biswas's life. The first section entitled 'Pastorals', describes the birth and childhood years of the protagonist but there is a simultaneous expression of the Hindu life in the customs, traditions, rituals and social philosophy of the people. There is a vivid presentation of the complete communal life in the characters like Bipti's father, who came to Trinidad as indentured labourers and reproduced an insulated India for themselves in Trinidadian surroundings. The superstitious beliefs, faith in pundits, adherence to rituals and above all their belief in preordination and bickering in values of Indianness make the novel a study of the disintegrating lives of the displaced Indians.

Mr. Biswas is born the wrong way with all the ill-omens and is six fingered. Immediately a pundit is called to see the child's horoscope and he makes dreadful predictions regarding the evils brought by this child on the family. After consulting his astrological almanac, the Pundit predicts. "**The boy will be a lecher and a spendthrift. Possible a liar as well........ Much of the evil this boy will undoubtedly bring**

will be mitigated if his father is forbidden to see him for twenty one days."[36]

Bissoondaye, Biswas's grandmother, follows Pundint's instructions diligently and it is only on the twenty-first day that Raghu has his first view of his son. Nevertheless, this ill-ominous child proves unlucky for Raghu and becomes the cause of his death. Bipti undergoes her initiation into widowhood in the traditional manner and rituals take place. The Indians have also retained their belief in destiny and fate. This is first expressed by Bipti's father when he consoles her about her unhappy marriage with Raghu by saying, "**Fate, there is nothing we can do about it.**"[37] It is also evident in the belief of the narrator himself who makes the following observation about Bipti's father : "**Fate had brought him from India to the sugar-estate, aged him quickly and left him to die in a crumbling mud but in the swamp lands**"[38]. Bipti too shows a passive resignation to fate till the end.

As a result of Raghu's death the family splits and disintegration takes its first turn when Bipti and Biswas have to move to Pagotes and live as dependants on Tara, Bipti's well-to-do-sister. The death of his father leaves Mr. Biswas homeless and emotionally bewildered and it is at this point that fragmentation of his life begins. The following passage reveals this fact:

> "And so Mr. Biswas came to leave the only house to which he had some right. For the next thirty-five years he was to be a wanderer with no place he could call his own, with no family except that which he was to attempt to create out of the engulfing world of the Tulsis. For with his mother's parents dead, his brother on the estate at Felicity, Dehuti as a servant in Tara's house, and himself rapidly growing away from Bipti, who, broken, became increasingly useless and impenetrable, it seemed to him that he was really quite alone."[39]

In Pagotes they live completely on Tara's charity. Bipti

loses her hold over Mr. Biswas because, by casting out his ill-tempered mother, he takes Tara as a mother substitute since everything is decided by her. It is Tara who sends him to the Canadian Mission school, and then suddenly decides that he should be made a pundit. Mr. Biswas begins his picars like journey through life after completing his primary education. Just as he is beginning to do stocks and shares, he is taken out to be groomed as a Hindu pundit under Pundit Jairam who himself is a strange man. He holds scandalous views and is full of contradictions :

> "He believed in God, fervently, but claimed it was not necessary for a Hindu to do so. He attacked the custom some family had of putting up a flag after a religious ceremony; but his own front garden was a veritable grove of bamboo poles with red and white pennants in varying stages of decay. He ate no meats but spoke against vegetarianism : 'when Lord Rama went hunting, did they think it was just for sport?."[40]

Mr. Biswas spends eight months with this eccentric man doing the mechanical side of Jairam's offices and copying out Sanskrit verses which he couldn't understand. Biswas is thrown out by Jairam because of a disgraceful act on his part and he returns to Pagotes. His mother, contrary to his hope of consoling, gets alarmed at his return and scolds him badly. Tara, again, sends him to help at her husband's rum shop which is being looked after by Bhandat, her brother-in-law. However, Bhandat considers Biswas as Tara's spy and takes a dislike for him because the boy has come as an intruder in his domain where he was spinning more coins everyday. He accuses Biswas of stealing a dollar and so beats him up and turns him out under this pretext Biswas returns once again and in his humiliation cries out pathetically, to his mother: "**Why do you keep on sending me to stay with other people.**"[41]

These sour experiences cause indelible scratches on the heart and mind of the protagonist and it is then that Biswas, for the first time declares his resolution to have his own house, which for him has become a symbol of liberation and identity "**I am going to get a job of my own. And am going to get my own house too. I am finished with this.**"[42] Now this boy is deeply enraged by his miserable predicament of non-entity and nothingness in life. After making a declaration of independence Biswas comes out to go on a search of his own-individual existence.

The life of Mr. Biswas takes a queer turn as he happens to meet his school mate Alec at a cafe in Pagotes where he is painting a sign board. Being a jobless derelict Biswas enters into a working partnership with Alec for sign painting. He develops a hobby also for reading and becomes addicted to Samuel Smiles and tries to identify with the heroes who, like himself, are young, poor and struggling. Yet he realises the vast difference between his condition and their's. The idea that colonial people are condemned to mediocrity underlies most of Naipaul's writings. Biswas, nevertheless attempts to rise above this mediocrity by trying to invent things but Trinidad cannot furnish him with the equipments necessary to carry out complex experiments. The novelist explains his wish in these words:

> "But he never ceased to worry. He no longer simply lived. He had begun to wait, not only for love but for the world to yield its sweetness and romance. He deferred all his pleasure in life until that day. And it was in this mood of expectation that he went to Hanuman House at Arwacas and saw Shama."[43]

Now the epic struggle of the protagonist against the domineering Tulsi clan begins and his quest for his own significance becomes a much more obsessing thought with him. The Hanuman House stands like an alien white fortress crowned with a statue of the benevolent monkey god Hanuman, in the High street of Arwacas. Tulsis have some reputation among Hindus as pious, conservative family. It is his sign-painting that brings Biswas into contact with Tulsis and he is trapped into a marriage without any dowry and is also expected to become a pet commodity of Tulsi because he has no money or position of his own. Biswas is expected to merge into insignificance like the other sons-in-laws of Tulsis, some of whose names even have been forgotten. When Govind, one of the sons-in-law, suggests that Biswas should give up sign-painting and become a driver in a Tulsi estate, Biswas immediately voices his dissent as: "**Give up sign-painting ? And my independence ? No boy. Motto is: Paddle you own canoe.**"[44] The rebellious nature of Biswas is regarded with hostility and so ridiculed but he is against the conformity-subsistence, master-slave syndrome so meticulously built-up and maintained by the Tulsi matriarch. As Gordon Rohlehr points out: "**Tulsidom depends for its existence on the psychic emasculation of the men and on the maintenance of their sense of inferiority.**"[45]

Biswas revolts against the rank negation of individuality and freedom; his anguish is channelised into expression of his abusive behaviour and foul language, e.g., his throwing of food out of the window on Owad's head; referring to Mrs. Tulsi as the 'old she fox', kicking the pregnant Shama, his wife in the belly etc. To insult the Tulsis he joins the Aryans, a group of revisionist Hindu Missionaries from India and preaches against all the doctrines held by Tulsi. Santosh Chakraborti explains this antagonistic situation as:

> "Biswas's antagonism to this emasculation is as intense as the Tulsi's antagonism to individualism is prompt. But Biswas's rebelliousness is not instinctive but inspired by the circumstantial constraints of entrapment. As soon as he feels that through his marriage in the Tulsi family he has bartered his freedom for security and that he is trapped, the only course left to him is escape - from entrapment to freedom, from ossifying existentiality to emotional release."[46]

The insight about his uncertainty and inconsequentiality of life makes Biswas realise that he has achieved nothing and so he becomes more quarrelsome. On one occasion, he goes to the extent of spitting on Owad for which he is beaten up by Govind and sent away to 'the Chase'. It prompts him to accept the order of Seth to go ahead and paddle his own canoe and his onward move to The Chase. The journey to the Chase begins the most significant chapter of his life—his quest for a house of his own as well as his first independent encounter with real life—though it ends in a failure. His shift to Tulsi shop at Chase releases him from the state of asphyxiation in the Tulsi household to the dynamic of struggle in the world outside.

However, from the beginning at 'The Chase' Biswas has the feeling that it is just a temporary arrangement—a pause, a preparation and the real life is to begin for him soon and elsewhere. Naipaul diagnoses the feeling of temporariness to be a typical condition among the displaced people. Even Hanuman House, for all its apparent solidity, is actually built of clay bricks; the house consists of a vast number of desperate families of displaced Indians brought under the Tulsidom by the economic needs. The Tulsis have never considered themselves finally settled in Arwacas or even in Trinidad. It is no more than a stage in the journey that had begun when Pundit Tulsi left India. So the fluidity of life is a reality of all Indians here and Tulsis are no exception to it.

After coming to the Chase Shama is quite unhappy on being separated from the protecting figure of Hanuman House. Mr. Biswas, though, gets a relief yet he is not able to overcome the feeling of nothingness and temporaries throughout his stay here. His loneliness makes him recall the bonding and noisy activities of Hanuman House where, in spite of all the hostility, he had been acknowledged at least as a clown. At 'The Chase' he feels to be reduced to non-entity as everything beyond the shop's gate is foreign and unimportant. Through this sense of realization by the protagonist. Naipaul seeks to convey that it is one's sense of relationship that is root of identity and the loss of relationship leads only to alienation. When Biswas realises that Hanuman House is a sanctuary he needs, he though unwillingly, improves his relationship with the Tulsis and also makes visits to the Hanuman House. Nevertheless, a vague sense of desolation and uncertainty still haunts him and heightens the tension between him and Shama. He is possessed with a fear psychosis and there is an inner crisis as he has yet to find his own place in an environment that disowns him. Biswas's first attempt to paddle his own canoe meet's with failure when his shop incurs heavy losses and he is forced to accept the job of a sub-overseer at a meagre salary of twenty five dollars, in one of the Tulsi estates at 'Green Vale.'

Life in a room at the barracks in 'Green Vale' is a harrowing experience for Biswas. There he feels suffocated, tired, sweating and insulted by working with labourers who treat him nothing more than a representative of Seth. He blames Shama's mother for all his miseries but Shama reacts by going back to the fold of Hanuman House with her son Anand. On one of his visits to Hanuman House Biswas sees Anand standing against the pillars and is reminded of the other boy he had once seen outside the hut at dusk. The vision sets Mr. Biswas in action and his house begins to take shape in reality. But Biswas's first attempt to claim a portion on the earth fails to bear fruit since the house meets the same end as the doll's house he had gifted to his daughter Savi on her birthday and by this reiteration of his independence he only annoyed Mrs. Tulsi. The house Mr. Biswas starts building at Green Vale can in no way be an embodiment of his aspirations, for he is still dependent on the Tulsis. Besides it the financial constraints compel him to make compromises and the house he manages to get constructed bears no resemblance to his dream house. He still suffers from a sense of nowherness and alienation and this intensity is reflected in his conversation with his son:

> "Who is your father?"
> 'You,'

> Wrong. I am not your father. God is you father'
> 'Oh, And what about you?'
> 'I am just somebody. Nobody at all. I am just a man you know."[47]

Mr. Biswas shifts into his one room house in a defiant gesture with the hope that living in his own house would bring about a change in the state of his mind. However, when his dog is brutally killed presumably by the dispossessed lobourers, Biswas is badly shaken and feels more threatened than ever. The same day he has a nervous breakdown and he is taken back to the Hanuman House for treatment. His miserable condition is described as:

> "When the man returned, dripping with Anand sleepily and tearfully walking beside them and Govind carrying Mr. Biswas in his arms, there was relief and some disappointment. Mr. Biswas was not wild or violent; he made no speeches; he did not pretend he was driving a motorcar or picking cocoa—the two actions popularly associated with insanity. He only looked deeply exasperated and fatigued."[48]

When he recovers, Seth breaks the news to Mr. Biswas that his house has been burnt down by the labourers and it frustrates him further. He recovers from depression after resting at Hanuman House and he could feel the relief in thinking that he has survived the horror. The one positive outcome of the time spent at Green Vale is that Biswas is able to claim his children, Savi and Anand, who had here-to-fore been the assets only of Hanuman House.

On recovering, Biswas reviews his situation once again and finds that "**He was the father of four children and his position was as it had been when he was seventeen, unmarried and ignorant of the Tulsis.**"[49] Inertia settles upon him once again and compels him to stay at the Hanuman House. He is goaded into action once again by congregating all his vigour when Seth tells him that Mrs. Tulsi and Owad are expected back from Port of Spain which means that he must vacate Owad's room. Biswas leaves quietly without seeing Shama and his fourth child. When he sets out he has no idea where to go and what to do. It is quite by chance that he gets into a bus going to Port of Spain and ends up as a journalist of *'Trinidad Sentinel.'*

The process of cultural disintegration takes a fast pace as we see that even Hanuman House also disintegrates. It is to be seen in their celebration of Christmas and more definitely in the arranged marriage of Tulsi's son Shekar with a Presbyterian Dorothy. We can not miss this change in socio-cultural priorities. Caste even religion, the prime considerations till the marriage of Mr. Biswas, have now been replaced by pecuniary factor. Shekar's marriage takes place in the registrar office after which instead of bringing the bride home, it is the groom who leaves Hanuman House to **"look after the cinema land and the filling station of his wife's family."**[50] We witness further decline of Tulsi family as within the Hanuman House quarrels ensue and beneath the external unity there are individualistic tendencies rising up. This household starts collapsing under the selfishness and greed of its inmates who have been deeply motivated by the western ideas of monetary gain and liberty. All this foretells that soon a complete collapse would occur at Shorthills.

The second part of the novel mainly focuses on Port of Spain where Mrs. Tulsi and Owad have shifted and Mr. Biswas also arrives after leaving Hanuman House. It is an adventure, an interlude as he gets foothold he has long been in search of. His job at *'Trinidad Sentinel'* establishes his identity as a person in his own right and it also changes the attitude of Tulsis towards him. So when the reconciliation takes place between him and Tulsis, it is on some terms that makes Biswas feel that he has won a victory. His relationship with Mrs. Tulsi becomes less formal while a sweet companionship grows between him and Owad. At times he even forgets that the house belongs to the Tulsis as the rose bush he plants in the garden testifies. But the disintegration of Tulsis and Seth's break-up with the Tulsis and Mrs. Tulsi's subsequent decision to shift to Shorthills also comes as blows to Biswas upsetting his routine once again.

At Shorthills with no Seth to supervise there is a complete split in Tulsis. Here everyone tries to exploit the resources to his own advantage. Govind and Tuttle are foremost in this plundering but Biswas also takes an advantage of his stay at Shorthills. Disunity sets in among the children as well and this is reflected in their bitter fights of pure hate. Naipaul exposes the shrewdness of Mr. Biswas in plundering:

> "Though surrounded by devastation, Mr. Biswas remained detached. He paid no rent; he spent nothing on food; he was saving most of his salary. For the first time he had money and every fortnight it was increasing. He closed his heart to sorrow and anger at a dereliction he was powerless to prevent; and recognising with a thrill that it was now everyman for himself—the phrase gave him much pleasure—he continued to plunder, enjoying the feeling that in the midst of chaos he was calmly going about his own devilish plan."[51]

Obviously there is no longer any cultural or communal unity and no Hanuman House to protect the Tulsis as well as their dependent Hindus. Everyone has to fight for oneself in a new world-the world Owad and Shekar have already entered. Hari, the family pundit also passes away and there is no other pundit to perform *puja* at Hanuman house. The disintegration of Hindu culture and odd assimilation into the Creole culture is complete when Mrs. Tulsi starts sending Sushila to burn candles in the Roman Catholic Church, puts a crucifix in her room and has Pundit Tulsi's grave cleaned for All Saint's Day.

Having saved a considerable amount of money while at Shorthills, Biswas is able to complete his new house and shifts into it. Built in wilderness this house is inconvenient and Biswas waits to be released from this location. Again he accepts the offer of Mrs. Tulsi to occupy two rooms in the Port of Spain. The feeling of instability and oppression still haunts him as this attempt to have his own house also proves another failure. In spite of all the negative aspects, however, it is in this house that for the first time the Biswases live together as a family. It is now that Biswas feels the responsibilities of a father and husband as well.

Once again Biswas sinks into despondency as he realises that still he has to achieve the life he wishes to live. Night after night he sinks but now there is no quickening panic or any knot of anguish. He discovers in himself only a great unwillingness. In this section of the novel the sudden economic boom created by the American presence is evidenced in the way people like Govind and Tuttle become suddenly rich. However, Biswas's economic position remains unchanged because he does not have access to this kind of money. Biswas continues to live in the Port of Spain house even after Owad returns from England. Owad's return revives the community life of the Tulsis and Biswas finds it very difficult even to sleep at this place. Then one day Owad slaps Anand for answering back and in his humiliation Anand appeals to his father that he can't bear to live in this house another day. Biswas who himself has faced such insult innumerable times, is deeply moved by his son's appeal; and in his own helplessness creates a scene. On the same night Biswas insults Mrs. Tulsi and on her notice declares to vacate her house at the earliest. Having committed himself Biswas sets about looking for a rentable accommodation because with a saving of eight hundred dollars, it is impossible to even think of buying a house. But when he gets four hundred dollars for his Shorthills house, he managed a loan of four thousand dollars from Ajodha and finally decides to purchase the solicitor's clerk's house at Sikkim Street in Port of Spain.

Though Shama is defiant and reluctant to leave the security fold of Tulsi family and is in sullen mood when taken to see the house, she settles down very soon after shifting to their new house. After moving into this house, Biswases discover its many flaws and realise that they have been cheated. Nevertheless, the fact that it is their own house makes them accommodate themselves to every peculiarity and awkwardness of the house. Naipaul comments on the enormity of this achievement:

> "Soon it seemed to the children that they had never lived anywhere but in the tall square house in Sikkim Street. From now their lives would be ordered, their memories coherent. The mind, while it is sound is merciful. And rapidly the memories of Hanuman House in Port of Spain would become jumbled, blurred; events would be telescoped, many forgotten. Occasionally a nerve of memory would be touched....."[52]

Now ultimately Biswas finds his own portion of land and is in his own house. Shama's new-found loyalties become evident in the way she prepares the house to receive the Tuttles, she even tells them, **"I don't want anything bigger. This is just right for me. Something small and nice.**"[53] Mr. Biswas too learns to reciprocate the feeling of love. Naipaul makes it clear that for displaced people like Biswases owning a house does not just mean having a shelter. It means imposition of an order into their chaotic and patternless existence. It signifies stability and coherence which are the pre-requisites for the carving of an authentic selfhood. In Madhusudan Rao's words:

> "In his own house, which is incomplete like his own syncopated individuality, he has come to respect the feeling of love—that state of consciousness which recognizes the value of gifting one's self away to meet another's human need. In a sense, Mr. Biswas has at last arrived."[54]

The quest for selfhood is the central force for this struggle. In this regard Dagmar Barnouw also writes:

> "To be housed permanently, one's privacy and dignity safeguarded, would become the largely elusive goal that derives Mr. Biswas. He finally does manage to acquire his house after several unsuccessful attempts, out here too, without noticing its many obvious problems. It would have been terrible for Mr. Biswas to die without his house amid the squalor of his wife's large disintegrating and indifferent family, even worse without any attempting to lay claim to one's portion of the earth; to have lived and died as one had been born unnecessary and unacommodated........ superfluous as no human being should be."[55]

Yet the house for Mr. Biswas does not redeem his terrible and ordinary fate. For a while he is successful as a journalist but his career is prematurely ended by the loss of his mentor. His one story 'Escape' remains a fragment and his nucleus family starts disintegrating as his son leaves him and will not be able to draw on his father's writing.

Soon Mr. Biswas dies of heart attack and his death is given the least importance. What is more important is that Biswas dies an accommodated man who has been successful in claiming a portion of the earth as his own and in leaving behind a proof of his existence. No doubt, the tragic vision of the novelist has reached its height in the Epilogue where all achievements of Mr. Biswas gradually start dissolving and the pride of authenticity changes into a deep sense of the absurdity and loss. Mr. Biswas dies as a neglected man, but now neglect comes from his own son for whom he is reduced to nothing more than just a somebody. However it is in the dignity of his death that Mr. Biswas's triumph lies.

Compared to the preceding three novels *'A House for Mr. Biswas'* demonstrates the picaresque like journey of rootless protagonist coming from the colonial situations and struggling to find a foothold in the New World. Naipaul deals sensitively with the colonial people's quest for order and identity. It is only natural that these displaced people are all in the predicament of Mr. Biswas as they find themselves out of place in alien land. The rebellion as well as quest in Mr. Biswas is defined by his state as a cultural, psychological and social orphan. So often his individual anguish is symbolic expression of the rage of the displaced Indians away from their real land and also of their alienation which leads them to sufferings due to a vehement denial of their individuality. Beneath the self-laceration and grotesque quest for selfhood lies a fear of the future, of objects, of people; of time, of place and of mankind., Biswsas is living to an extreme degree with the anxieties of the uprooted man and his elaborate poses, day dreams, assertion of self and evasion of responsibility are all results of the cultural, social and psychological 'nowhereness' produced by his position as a second generation poor Hindu in Trinidad.

'A House for Mr. Biswas', culminates the first phase of Naipaul's artistic development. Here he is particularly interested in the colonised people's quest for identity and the fate of individuals in the colonial situation is the main theme. Compared to the proceeding three novels it demonstrates a fulness of character development and attainment of a selfhood. Naipaul's masterly craftsmanship lies in the fact that he has been able to present a hero in all his littleness and still preserves a sense of the man's inner dignity. Viewed against the background of the East Indian Trinidadian society in disintegration, Biswas is a picaroon and his achievements are heroic.

We may make common cause with Francis Wyndham who says that: **"*A House for Mr. Biswas* is as subtle and comprehensive an analysis of the colonial situation as anything in the imaginative literature."**[56] Biswas is only forty-six when he dies, but by the end of the novel a whole history has passed before our eyes. The individual's sense of being comes from his social existence and in order to forge an authentic personality there is individual's confrontation against society that vehemently denies it.

References

1. Ashis Nandy, Preface to *'The Intimate Enemy : Loss and Recovery of Self under Colonialism'* (Delhi : Oxford University Press, 1983), p. xi.
2. V.S. Naipaul, *'The Mystic Masseur'* (London : Picador-an imprint of Pan Macmillan Ltd. 2002) p. 8.
3. *Ibid.,* p. 9.
4. *Ibid.,* p. 10.
5. *Ibid.,* p. 15.
6. Harihar Rath and K.C. Mishra, 'The Mystic Masseur : A study in Third World Politics, *V.S. Naipaul: Critical Essay'* vol. I, (edit.) Mohit K. Ray (New Delhi; Atlantic Publishers and Distributors, 2002), p. 18.
7. V.S. Naipaul, *'The Mystic Masseur'* op. cit., p. 11.
8. Harihar Rath & K.C. Mishra, op. cit., p. 22.
9. Champa Rao Mohan, *Postcolonial Situation in the Novels of V.S. Naipaul* (New Delhi: Atlantic Publishers and Distributors, 2004), p. 33.
10. V.S. Naipaul, *'The Suffrage of Elvira'* (Harmondsworth : Penguin, 1969) p. 80.
11. *Ibid.,* p. 34.
12. *Ibid.,* p. 46.
13. *Ibid.,* p. 73.
14. *Ibid.,* p. 24.
15. *Ibid.,* p. 13.
16. *Ibid.,* p. 196-197.
17. *Ibid.,* p. 66.
18. *Ibid.,* p. 114.
19. Idem.
20. See quoted in Champa Rao Mohan's *Postcolonial Situations in the Novels of V.S. Naipaul* op. cit., p.41.
21. George Lamming, *'The Pleasures of Exile'*, (London : Michael Joseph, 1960) See quoted in Champa Rao Moham, *op. cit.* p. 42.

22. V.S. Naipaul, *'The Suffrage of Elvira'* op. cit., p. 206.
23. Yashoda Bhat, *V.S. Naipaul: An Introduction,*(New Delhi: B. R. Publishing Corporation, 2000), p. 69.
24. Bibhu Padhi, *Naipaul on Naipaul and the Novel; Modern Fiction Studies;* 30.3 (1984) p.495.
25. V.S. Naipaul, *'Miguel Street'*, (London : Andre Deutsch, 1959), p. 163.
26. V.S. Naipaul, *'The Middle Passage'* (Harmondsworth : Penguin. 1969), p.82.
27. V.S. Naipaul, *'Miguel Street'*, op. cit., p. 190.
28. *Ibid.*, p. 111.
29. *Ibid.*, p. 68.
30. *Idem.*
31. *Ibid.*, p. 69.
32. *Ibid.*, p. 115.
33. *Ibid.*, p. 216.
34. Bruce F. MacDonald, 'Symbolic Action in Three of V.S. Naipaul's Novels; *Journal of Commonwealth Literature* 9, No. 3 (April 1975) p. 243.
35. Robert D. Hamner, (edit) *'Character and Setting; Critical Perspectives on V.S. Naipaul* (London :1979), pp. 213-214.
36. V.S. Naipaul, *'A House for Mr. Biswas'* (London : Picador—an imprint of Pan Macmillan Ltd. 2005), p. 12-13.
37. *Ibid.*, p.11.
38. *Idem.*
39. *Ibid.*, p.38.
40. *Ibid.*, 49.
41. *Ibid.*, p. 64.
42. *Ibid.*, p. 66.
43. *Ibid.*, p. 80.
44. *Ibid.*, p. 108.
45. See Gordon Rohlehr, *'The Ironic Approach; Critical Perspective'*. quoted in Champa Rao Mohan's 'Postcolonial Situation in the Novels of V.S. Naipaul', op. cit., p. 62.

46. Santosh Chakraborti, 'Naipaul's Discourse of Aspiration'; *V.S. Naipaul Critical Essays*, Vol. I, (edit) Mohit K. Ray, op.cit., p. 41.
47. V.S. Naipaul, *'A House for Mr. Biswas'*, op.cit., p. 291.
48. *Ibid.*, p. 307.
49. *Ibid.*, p. 317.
50. *Ibid.*, p. 24.
51. *Ibid.*, p. 430.
52. *Ibid.*, p. 614.
53. *Ibid.*, p. 613.
54. Madhusudan Rao, *'Contrary Awareness: A Critical Study of the Novels of V.S. Naipaul* (Guntur Sardhi, 1982), p. 99.
55. Dagmar Barnouw, *'Naipaul's Strangers'* (Bloomington: Indiana University Press, 2003), p. 32.
56. Francis Wyndhan, *'V.S. Naipaul; Listener'*, (7 Oct. 1971), p. 462.

4

Postcolonial Chaos and Paradox of Freedom and Power in the Third World Nations

> *"We lack order. Above all we lack power and we do not understand that we lack power."*[1]
>
> *– V.S. Naipaul*

With the writings of his early novels V.S. Naipaul raised his own problem of displacement and loss and by reconstructing his personal experiences into the fictional form, he also attempted to come to terms with his own rootlessness and exile. The problem has, to some extent, been resolved with the writing of *'A House for Mr. Biswas'* for although, Naipaul still could not lay claim to his portion of earth as such, yet he has at least established his own identity. It is in the next phase of Naipaul 's career, which began with a travelogue *'The Middle Passage'* (1962), that an attempt has been made to analyse his reactions to the postcolonial scenario all around the world. Writing of *'A House for Mr. Biswas'* had been like a career for Naipaul but it had left him artistically enervated. He had begun to realize too that "it

wasn't easy for the exotic writer to get his work accepted as being more than something exotic."[2]

It was, in part, to get rid himself of the fear of artistic sterility as well as his desire to be something more than a regional writer that led him to write *' Mr. Stone and Knight's Companion'* (1963). It helped him to cut across the regional boundaries and secure a place for himself among the writers of the world stream. The novel deals with exclusively English characters in an exclusive English setting and does not have any immediate concern with the colonial or postcolonial Third World societies. So, it is excluded from the purview of this study. Naipaul's further novels as well as his travelogues which reiterate the thematic aspects of the postcolonial situation in the slave countries are the main source of his power as a writer.

As an exile enmeshed in the cultural collisions of his epoch, Naipaul does not escape their disintegrating and alienating effects. His dislocation from his roots enables him to treat his own alienation as an instance of his quest for identity of colonial and postcolonial peoples. Like a versatile exile, he pursues the middle passage by living in between and through this non-aligned sharing of both origins and ends, he strives to discover his centre. Consequently Naipaul has always felt physical distance from his subject for an objective presentation of his material. So travel, indeed, proved to be an important stimulus for the further development of his art. These travels not only helped Naipaul to enrich his insight perceptions but also to overcome his uncertainties and to achieve the clarity of vision. It were only his travels which broadened Naipaul's perspective and made it possible for him to view his personal emptiness and homelessness against the wider context of the larger world. These travels across the world shifted his emptiness from the earlier preoccupations of rather personal nature to the broader and more general themes that emerged in his later works. In correlating his travel writings with his fiction, there is an obvious and constant feedback between both travel and fictional paradigms in his texts.

The objective of travel writings has been much like the objective of anthropological and ethnographic fieldwork reporting : the faithful portrayal of the 'other' that is the Third World marginal groups like ethnic and racial minorities whether they are in the developing nations or are floating in the first world. The textualising of these travel experiences by the writer has been, no doubt, conditioned by the centre ideologies that fit into the paradigms of the new world for the colonizers and the colonized. Moreover, it is hard to ascertain, like the proverbial chicken and the egg which would come first; whether the fictional element in his travel narratives or the travel paradigms in his fiction. In 1960 he began to travel and '*The Middle Passage*' (1962) records his impressions of colonial society in the West Indies and South America. Naipaul is a person on the margins by inheritance and choice. To him the history of the islands can never be satisfactorily told and as such **"history is built around achievement and creation; and nothing was created in the West Indies."**[3] '*The Middle Passage*' treats the enduring effects of Caribbean Societies' histories of imperial depredations and depletion and colonial marginality:

> "The Caribbean has been described as Europe's other sea, the Mediterranian of the New World . It was a Mediterranian which summoned up every dark instinct without the complementary impulses towards nobility and beauty of older lands, a Mediterranian where civilization turned Satanic, perverting those it attracted. And if one considers this sea, which the tourist enlivens in his fantastic uniform , as a wasteful consumer of men through more than three centuries – the aboriginal population of some millions wiped out; the insatiable plantations: 300,000 slaves taken to Surinam which today has a Negro population of 90,000; the interminable wars ; 40,000 British soldiers dead between 1794 and 1796 alone, and another 40,000 discharged as unfit – it would seem that simply to have survived in the West Indies is to have triumphed."[4]

This travelogue is about the clients and customers who have consumed human beings by turning them to slaves and indentured workers—Amerindians, African slaves, Asian indentured labourers, and European colonists, soldiers and missionaries. Naipaul is certainly caricaturing a culture to comprehend his own exile and his own marginality of existence. Citing Aime Cesaire, James Clifford contends that mimicry can also turn into syncretism, a construction of a new identity:

> "The Caribbean history from which Cesaire derives an inventive and tactical 'negritude' is a history of degradation, mimicry, violence and blocked possibilities and (yet) it is also rebellious, syncretistic and creative. This kind of ambiguity keeps the planet's local futures uncertain and open. There is no master narrative that can reconcile the tragic and comic plots of global cultural history."[5]

Besides documenting the dirt and squalor of the colonial people, '*The Middle Passage*' records the failure of the colonial Trinidadians and West Indians too to discover their roots, to find a viable centre for their existence. There is an important difference between the self and other relationship in European colonial discourse and in Naipaul's discourse on the West Indies and the Caribbean. In the former, the European self-reduces the colonial other to an object, an entity devoid of an 'I'; because colonial subjectivity has been denied, there can only be a hollow colonial mimicry of the European self. In the latter discourse, the author as exile who returns temporarily to the Caribbean, is torn between conflicting aspects of his own identity; the colonial subject can't be made to disappear because, in a sense, Naipaul is himself, the subject of his own travels and critique. Unable to deny the colonial self, he wrestles with his malaise.

The book portrays an anguished quest for an understanding of the fragmented self. Naipaul diagnoses the problems of the marginal man—uncertainty of identity, feelings of inferiority, scorn for one's own culture and society. It echoes European colonial discourse and at the same time does away with the western stereotyped images of the Caribbean as a tropical paradise. There is a new urge and potentiality in motion since with the collapse of the colonial's dislocation and of the centrality of experiences, it makes visible the peripheries wherein the exile moves. Thus the book, besides being an autobiography of the author himself, is an exile's break with the center and a perception from the margins of other worlds where things are never seen whole but only broken and twisted against themselves.

'*An Area of Darkness*' (1964), Naipaul's second travelogue, follows the model created by him in '*The Middle Passage*'. It is a different variation of the formula he developed in the first one. The book does not just express his anthropological, sociological, historical and ethnographic observations, views and discussions; it is also a work of great introspective reflection. His visit to India was similar in a way to his visit to the West Indies. Although Naipaul had never visited India earlier, his first visit in the sixties was preceded by the romantic notions and stories on which he was fed in the West Indies by his immigrant relatives. His visit to India was perhaps motivated by his desire to explore his roots and redefine his position as a Hindu of Indian origin; he wished to examine quietly whether India could be his home; since the Caribbean islands could not be.

On the basis of the romantic picture of India embedded deep in his consciousness he had come to the '*dream land*' of his ancestral roots with high expectations. Perhaps he had desired to see a revitalized, rejuvenated India but simultaneously preserving the ancient culture as well. His visits to Trinidad and India—both countries now learning with a postcolonial scenario had certain things in common. Naipaul finds that Indians like the West Indies people mimic the British and there is an inversion of freedom and power in this country also. However, the greatest difference between the two was that Trinidadians like Indians did not have the asset of rich ancient, pluralistic culture which was both an asset as well as a handicap in modernization. His double alienation was complete—the alienation from Trinidad and the one from India. He concludes in an *'Area of Darkness'*. **"It was a journey that ought not to have been made, it had broken my life in two."**[6]

He is a very inquisitive ethnographer and observes India with an imperialistic outlook of an outsider as well as an insider's sensitivity. He comes to the country with expectations but also with a sense of humiliation that his ancestors had to leave the motherland as indentured labourers. It is a striking feature of both *'An Area of Darkness'* and *'India: A Wounded Civilization'* that very often he starts with an objective narration emphasising the external details butthis facet gets superseded by his introspective and autobiographical projections. To him India was an area of darkness and he had come with the intention of discovering India. It is but natural, therefore, that his travelogue should be characterized by the expression of his brooding and probing. India becomes a resting place for his imagination. Quite a big chunk of his autobiography can be reconstructed from his travelogues - *'An Area of Darkness'*, *'The Enigma of Arrival'*, etc.

India was the background of Naipaul's childhood and ever since then India was the country of his imagination; known through the language he spoke at home with the immigrant Indians among whom he lived there and the books he read. To him India:

> "....was a country out in the void beyond the dot of Trinidad; and from it our journey had been final. It was a country suspended in time, it could not be related to the country discovered later—and I thought of the time when the transference was made as a period of darkness, darkness which also extended to the land, as darkness surrounds a hut at evening though for little way around the hut there is still light. The light was the area of my experience in time and place. And even now though time has widened,

> though space has contracted and I have travelled lucidly over that area which was to me the area of darkness, something of darkness in those attitudes, those ways of thinking and seeing, which are no longer mine."[7]

It was with such a background that Naipaul travelled to India and he wanted to explore the possibilities of finding his roots in India. As he travelled towards India through Cairo and other eastern countries, the East tried **"to reveal itself and each recognition was a discovery."**[8] And the first thing he discovered about India was that the India he had known was only a land of his imagination; it was an imaginary homeland.

Naipaul's predicament in India is very peculiar. In Trinidad and in London, Naipaul had learnt to have a distinctive existence. He had lived for years feeling different always because of his intellectual superiority. 'Difference' everywhere seems to be the essential keynote of his existence and discovery of it in India; a land of his childhood dreams was not without a shock and agony. 'Difference' is the essence of post modernism and Naipaul has a claim to it; he is a 'postmodern' in life. He is a very severe critic of life in India; for instance he criticizes the Indian films, the lack of hygiene in India and the religious practices which he finds meaning less. Naipaul is a born non-believer and finds that there is a wide gap between the high spiritual claims and the low, decadent, almost spiritually bankrupt everyday life in India which he came across and a life which he describes with illustrations.

Having grown up in a colonial country Naipaul is used to a colonial way of life and while he visits India he is in another colonial country and compares colonial Trinidad with colonial India. In Trinidad the colonial experiences, according to Naipaul, had not to be superimposed on an ancient civilization and so the experiences did not appear to be incongruous. So far the British encounter in India was concerned Naipaul writes. "**The England of India was totally**

different. It remained an incongruous imposition."[9] He is very severe in criticising when he says that the meeting of England and India was not fruitful; rather it was a violation. He writes **"The Indo-British encounter was abortive; it ended in a double fantasy. Their new self-awareness makes it impossible for Indians to go back, their cherishing of Indianness makes it difficult for them to go ahead....the creative urge failed."**[10] Naipaul observes that in this colonial experience, having lost the creativity, Indian minds only imitated the British and even looked at themselves through British eyes. "**It is still through European eyes that India looks at her ruins and her art. Nearly every Indian who writes on Indian art feels bound to quote from the writings of European admirers.**"[11] Even though Naipaul lived in India for a year, he could not understand India at all. He writes: " **In a year I had not learned acceptance. I had learned my separateness from India, and was content to be a colonial, without a past, without ancestors.**"[12] India eludes him and as he flies away from here and reaches Beirut, he observes: **"India was part of the night, a dead world, a long-journey."**[13]

Naipaul's severe criticism of India seems to be perhaps the result of his too short a stay in India for the stupendous nature of the enquiry in which Naipaul had engaged himself. A more patient attempt and perhaps more contact with people involved in such pursuits might have yielded a different and a better picture of India to him. He knows no Indian language and his communication with Indians was inadequate. Moreover, he carries his own prejudices as a Trinidad colonial in his attempt to understand India. His observation that India-England encounter was fruitless is also not wholly true. If India lost her creativity in the process, it is because of the British exploitation of India; it is something of a miracle that the spirit of India could survive at all. So far as the technological revolution is concerned it would have come to India even otherwise because it was a global phenomenon. Because of the contact with the British it came to us a little earlier with or without the intention of the British rulers.

Naipaul's dialogue with India continued when he visited India for the second time in 1975 and his second book about India was published in 1977, *'India : A Wounded Civilization'*. The initial shock to his imaginative, romantic fantasy about India and the acute sense of shame due to his ancestors' flight from their motherland as indentured labourers now receded a bit and therefore the narrator of this travelogue relies less on the memory and the stranger's eye. Naipaul now has a professional rather than a personal mandate to fulfill but his personal history still remains the foundation on which he builds this book. As earlier, a general handicap he has insufficient communication with people and is ignorant of Indian languages through which to communicate to them. Besides he carries all along with him a backlog of his prejudices and his imperial stances. However *'India: A Wounded Civilization'* is much more thoughtful and reflective than *'An Area of Darkness'*.

Moreover, Naipaul's travels proved an important stimulus for the further growth of his art and vision. Undoubtedly, his travels have broadened his perspective as he could view his personal homelessness and existential absurdity against the wider context of the larger world. This resulted in widening the vision of Naipaul from personal to general themes in the fast changing world. Efforts to capture one's past cultural existence and the ancestral home are at the center of these travels but his novels present the crises of the incompetent half-made societies of the Third World more realistically.

'The Mimic Men' (1967) marks an important landmark in the literary career of V.S. Naipaul. Whereas, his early novels are preoccupied with the author's personal experiences' articulation into fictional form to come to terms with his own displacement, *'The Mimic Men'* combines autobiography as well as the politics to expose especially the predicament of a country in post-colonial era striving to develop its own independent system and abilities to sustain its existence. Here again Naipaul's main themes are; the escape of the Third

World into fantasy on being poverty-ridden and isolated on the fringes of power; the sprouting up of various political and religious movements which though ineffective, offer a sense of excitement but end in despair and appeal to race and colour. The absence of real power, culture and competence has resulted in a tendency to mimic and in a feeling of meaninglessness, inferiority and non-entity.

The immigrants are still trapped in their unbreakable colonial situations but the independence has caused more gruesome disturbances in their lives and this makes these novels quite sad, bleak, seriousand reflective. The early gaiety and mockery is now replaced by a morose despair which is effectively conveyed in the grim and humourless tone of these novels. Naipaul's vision of the world, henceforth becomes progressively bleak and the tone becomes more and more penetrating. Champa Rao Mohan writes in this connection :

> "The themes of alienation, homelessness and mimicry still preoccupy Naipaul but the perspective has changed. They are now viewed as a universal condition of the modern world afflicting both colonized and colonizers alike. Besides the familiar themes that still haunt Naipaul's pen, there are themes that appear for the first time – the broader post-colonial themes of power and freedom and neocolonialism."[14]

Naipaul's novel *'Mr. Stone and the Knight's Companion'* (1963) is excluded from this study since it deals with exclusively English characters in an exclusive English setting and does not have any immediate concern with the Third World societies. The novels which reiterate the predicament of the postcolonial Third World societies and their immigrants on alien lands present an interrelation and continuity of themes dealt with in the first four novels. Thus *'The Mimic Men'* (1967), *'A Flag on the Island'* (1967) and *'In a Free State'* (1971) set the forthcoming seriousness and poignancy which portray the newly independent colonies and their critical situations. While the displaced colonials of the earlier novels cherished England as the land of opportunities and escape to England meant an escape from all miseries in *'The Mimic Men'*, London is exposed for what it is—a mirage, a mere illusion - and the promised land turns out to be equally fraudulent. Thematic continuity is further maintained through a much more comprehensive treatment of the concept of identity for with political independence the strife for power and a search for identity has become a more complex affair within the strange socio-political situations. Naipaul now seems to be concerned with the rootlessness and placelessness of a typical modern alone man,—the colonial individual in his predicament of nowhereness and loss of identity.

It would also be relevant to establish a connection between the narrator protagonist of *"The Mimic Men"* and V.S. Naipaul the author himself. While in the preceding novels Naipaul maintained his separateness from his characters through the use of irony in *'The Mimic Men'* however, he makes no attempt to maintain such separate identity. Ralph Singh, the protagonist—narrator is very close to Naipaul and at no point in the novel Singh becomes the target of author's irony. In *'The Mystic Masseur'* there was the narrator's version contradicting Ganesh's version to guide our responses. In *'Miguel Street'* we find the dichotomy of the dual perspective of the narrator as a boy and as an adult to highlight the ironies. The absence of such manipulations in *'The Mimic Men'* leads one to conclude that Ralph Singh and Naipaul are one. Naipaul's concern with his own self-occupies a major portion of his literary output and *'The Mimic Men'* is no exception to it. The autobiographical portion covers his early days in England, his meeting Sandra, his marriage and the breaking up of it. The merger of identities is further underscored by the fact that many of Naipaul's attitudes and tastes have been transferred on to R. Singh. Even Sandra, Singh's English wife is modelled on Laraine, an American girl whom Naipaul met during his pilgrimage to Amarnath. Singh, thus seems to represent Naipaul and his reconciliation to his lot signifies Naipaul's own reconciliation to his displacement. Kavita Nandan in her article *' Exile in The Mimic Men'* writes:

> "The representation of MM (sick) of the fractured diasporic colonized subject is a critique of the colonial project of modernization / progress that was based on the metaphysics of presence/permanence in which the self was regarded as whole, stable and rational."[15]

The novel begins with Ralph Singh, an exiled or rather a withdrawn politician, fatigued by disillusion rather than failure, writing his memories in an aseptic, placeless London suburb. The protagonist—the narrator—is the representative of a generation which gains power at independence and could only mimic their colonial authorities. The escapist tendency of the author as well as the people of the new world results in the creation of the character called Ralph Singh. The strong Hindu foundation of his life is revealed here and his romantic fancy world is full of Rajputs, Aryans as well as stories of knights. His disillusionment and disgust with the world in which he lived finds an unambiguous expression: **"We pretended to be real, to be learning, to be preparing ourselves for life. We mimic men of the New World, with all its corruption that come so quickly to the new."**[16]

This political biography transcends from the level of a personal, confessional report to an existential allegory of the modern man. Ralph Singh's various failures at the level of personal life are indicative of a larger national failure. The social analysis which Naipaul attempts in *'The Mimic Men'* is not confined even to the West Indies but extends to the entire Third World:

> "It was my hope to give expression to the restlessness, the deep disorder, which the great explorations, the overthrow in three continents of established social organizations, the unnatural bringing together of peoples.... But this work will not now be written by me; I am too much a victim of that restlessness which

> was to have been my subject. And it must also be confessed that in that dream of writing I was attracted less by the act and the labour than by the calm and the order which the act would have implied."[17]

Ralph Singh struggles like an artist to create something, to discover some meaning in the muddled state of affairs which his life has been. The story he records can be described as tracing Ralph Singh's transition from innocence to experience and his passage from the external disorder to personal harmony. In the opinion of K.I. Madhusudan Rao: **"The writing of his story becomes the very means to endure the terror, shipwreck abandonment and loneliness of his situation—."**[18] By analysing and interpreting his own experiences he hopes to find some order within the chaos of the present, and the uncertainty of the future in the contemporary colonial society. There is much in his wrecked life to reckon with; an uneasy childhood, a painful youth, a broken marriage, an abortive political career. Living alone in a suburban London hotel room, the narrator-protagonist, drawing on his memory, attempts to salvage his wrecked life to reconstruct the meaning of his life. So the novel is not in the form of a linear, chronological memoir commenting about the narrative technique of the novel. William Walsh observes that it is **"dissolving and non-linear in corresponding with the instrument of self-examination."**[19] The self-imposed order endows him with a freedom from the restrictions of sequential narration and also enables him to muse upon his childhood experiences dispassionately and analytically with an adult mind. While in the second part Singh reverts back to his childhood, in the final section of the novel he gives an account of his political career.

The narrator, a disgraced politician, is found recording his new impressions of London which are quite contrary to what he felt in the past shortly after the war. He writes about his student days, his marriage to an English girl, Sandra, his return to Isabella and his success in the world of business, politics and the ultimate debacle. Singh confesses that while at Isabella the island of his birth, he had been painfully aware of his ambiguous background: **"To be descended from generations of idlers and failures an unbroken line of the unimaginative, unenterprising and oppressed had always seemed to me to be a cause of deep, silent shame."** [20] Though Ralph Singh is busy analysing his own experiences and actions, he seems to achieve universality in describing the predicament of modern postcolonial existence. And later **"To be born on an island like Isabella, an obscure new world transplantation, secondhand and barbarous, was to be born to disorder."**[21] With such impressions in his mind about his island society, he comes to London, the great city of miraculous light, seeking order extension of himself. But now with all the experiences and affairs in this city, he seems to be completely disillusioned regarding the sustaining powers of London, **"the content of the world in which fleeing disorder, I had hoped to find the beginning of order."**[22]

Naipaul conveys the idea that identity is a feeble entity for colonials and this frustration of Singh is revealed in many of his outbursts. Singh first gets this insight when his grandfather is insulted by some labourers. Though they are just labourers, this insult deeply hurts Singh's grandfather and Ralph Singh gets his first political lesson, **"A man was only what he saw of himself in others."**[23] To get rid of this inner emptiness he begins to visit brothels. Being on the verge of a mental breakdown and in a distressed state he wanders aimlessly and suddenly meets Sandra at the school notice board. This incidental meeting later ends up in their marriage. Ralph Singh is attracted by the aura of good luck about her as well as her sense of sureness and precision which he himself lacks. Singh lists out the various things about Sandra that have fascinated him. Language was one of the foremost things. **"She was English. With her the mere fact of communication was a delight."**[24] Then comes her isolated state similar to his own and her aversion to commonness; **"She had no community, no group and had rejected her family. She was herself alone in the world**

and was determined to fight her way up. She hated the common."[25] Singh sees the magnitude of her social ambition which attracts him more and more and he comes to feel that with her resourcefulness and avidity, she could guide him through life's uncertainty. With too many expectations and a lot of confidence and self-assurance he leaves for Isabella in a mood of celebration hoping to set right the ruined pieces of his life through a new relationship in the bond of marriage.

Once on the island, all his hopes and dreams turn into nothing. His mother disapproves his marriage with a foreign girl. She creates an embarrassing scene by refusing to accept Sandra and the resultant hostility makes them land in a hotel instead of going home. Singh's gesture of rebellion against social convention thus, invites rejection not only on the domestic front but also from the society which leaves him isolated and wrecked. Writing about the post war Isabella, Paul Theroux observes: **"The initial seeming warmth, acceptance and approval gradually disappeared in course of time for Isabella is an instable, shallow, mixed and chaotic society."**[26]

At this juncture Singh becomes aware of the artificial cosmopolitanism present even on the island and diverts all his energies to his work and makes a fortune by developing the land his grandfather has left for him. The township is named *'Kripalville'* after his father and later on, ironically enough, it gets corrupted into *'Cripple Villi.'* Success comes to him in the form of wealth and now Singh and Sandra attach themselves to a neutral fluid group of young men who have studied abroad and have fantastically cosmopolitan wives and girlfriends. In this social circle, he experiences a solidity feeling for the first time and his character is not **"what others took it to be, but something personal and ordained."**[27] However, these things in no way, are capable of easing the psychological tensions and uncertainties growing between husband and wife. Soon, the island life begins to tire Sandra and she withdraws into her shell. Both of them drift away from one another finding cheap amorous pleasure in having affairs outside the wedlock. Even the enthusiasm with which they began to build Roman house vanishes and in spite of its house warming ceremony it leads to disastrous collapse of their marital life. At the climax of the ceremony, the deliberate destruction of some old things no longer required, stands out as a symbol of the chaotic and destructive leanings of the people of Isabella. Singh later reflects that it was the barrenness of their relationship which promised no growth but led to the rift between them. He, nevertheless, holds himself responsible for not doing anything to save the marriage. Sandra takes the ultimate step by leaving the island. Just before leaving Singh for good, she leaves a note saying, **"The Niger is a tributary of that Seine,"**[28] which makes the racial barrier, the discrepancy between husband and wife glaringly evident.

With England and his English wife having failed to cement the cracks in his wrecked life, Singh turns to India as the center of his dreams. He goes to the Aryan culture imagining it to be his own to explain his experiences:

> "How right our Aryan ancestors were to create gods..... The larger erotic dream, the god has eluded us. It is, whenever, moving out of ourselves we look for extensions of ourselves. We seek the physical city and find only a conglomeration of private cells."[29]

Naipaul does not portray Singh's experiences as that of a West Indies person but as that of a typical modern man who might be confronted anywhere in this world. It is noteworthy to view the opinion of N. Rama Devi in this regard:

> "Through Ralph Singh he (Naipaul) depicts man as living in constant fear of change, insignificance and alienation. Here the character attempts to escape into an ideal static vision of the self in the crystallization of experience."[30]

But the final responsibility for order lies with individual

and not with the society. The individual must face his own reality instead of escaping and failure comes only when moving out of ourselves we look for extensions of ourselves. With this realization Ralph Singh attempts to make sense out of his exile in order to overcome his fear of life. In doing so he recalls the days of his childhood and adolescence with the hope of discovering some meaning from his childhood experiences by arranging his life's incidents in a sequential order. In second part we have a clear picture, though in an embryonic form of the maladies and evils which are later to loom large over the postcolonial settings. They are the tendency of the children to mimic their eagerness to disown their past and escape from their present realities. This terrifying anomaly of the situation can be explained as the consequence of the disorder and inauthenticity imposed by the center on the margins of empire.

Encouraged by Browne his former school friend, Ralph Singh embarks on his political career. Browne, who is now the editor of '*The Socialist*', plans to celebrate the anniversary of the dock workers' exodus from the city as the first gesture towards independence and urges Singh to contribute the main article about his father. The article is written and with the publication of the anniversary issue of '*The Socialist*' their political movement gets launched. They win the election and Browne becomes the prime minister whereas Singh is made a cabinet minister. On coming to power Singh comes to realize the futility inherent in the new world politicians' situation. His failure to bring about the nationalisation of the sugar estates provokes racial riots and he is forced to make his escape to London. While writing his memoirs Singh reflects on his political career and comes to understand the fraudulence of power in the emergent Third World nations. The career of the new politicians of these nations is powerless and short-lived as portrayed in the following passage:

> "Politics for us are a do - or - die, once for all charge. Once we are committed we fight more than political battles; we often fight quite literally for our lives. Our

> transitional or makeshift societies do not cushion us. There are no universities or city houses to refresh us and absorb us after the heat of battle. For those who lose, and nearly everyone in the end loses, there is only one course flight. Flight to the greater disorder, the final emptiness. London and the home countries."[31]

This detail account given by Singh has identically happened in newly freed twenty islands i.e. ex-colonies. What is required by the governments of such countries is a sound policy but the election through mob has become only a mimic drama there. It was only later that they came to realise that the mob without skills was unproductive, offered nothing and having no power at all. Under such circumstances even a sincere politician can do nothing. This is the reason that Singh's party is unable to expel the white expatriates from the island as it was a promise made in their election agenda. The Third World nations lack even the local expertise and continue to depend on the imperial powers for technologies and financial aids. Champa Rao Mohan observes on this issue as:

> "Through Singh Naipaul draws attention to the neocolonialism to which the emergent nations fall victim because of their dependence on outside power. The economy thus suffers due to the manipulations of foreign investors. Industrialization in such countries is bound to end up as no more than a process of filling imported tubes and tins with various imported substances."[32]

So the independence in Third World nations is nothing more than a mockery. The crux of the problem is identified in the nature of the society itself and what exists is not a society but a kind of controlled chaos. The postcolonial politicians deluded the people into believing that only semblance was order and what there politicians actually did was all just antithetical. So after the brilliant success of '*A House for Mr. Biswas*', '*The Mimic Men*' is rather a pale production and its links with the earlier novels add to the intensity and completion of the postcolonial picture of the Third World.

However, in spite of all the images of shipwreck *'The Mimic Men'* is one of the optimistic novels of Naipaul's later works. At the end of the novel Singh has come to understand and accept the finality of his displacement and is now well-equipped to begin afresh. It is not only about the island's corrupt politicians that Ralph Singh enlightens the readers but also about the predicament of the newly independent people who are in a situation which only perpetuates the bastard status of their new world. The basic deficiency of the society is articulated through the narrator—protagonist and it exposes the illusions, conflicts and the vague objectives of the politics of the ex-colonies and it in fact, makes these people mimics.

Naipaul's next work *'A Flag on the Island'* is a collection of short stories. However, the title story is closer in form to the novella than to the short story or even the long short story. Madhusadan Rao observes in this regard: **"*A Flag on the Island* is something more than a long short story; it tends to be a novella with a tensely regulated movement of action, culminating in a symbolic finish."**[33]

'The Mimic Men' and *'A Flag on the Island'* overlap each other and there is a close affinity in the themes and structures of the two works. Both picturise the chaotic situation of the post-colonial societies that have become newly independent and both have the same trepidation in their thematic perspectives and structure. However, while the earlier one examines the paradox of freedom and power in relation to the post-colonial politicians, the later one illustrates the confusion that prevails in the post-colonial societies. One more important difference is that Frankie, the first person narrator—protagonist in *'A Flag on the Island'*, being an American is an outsider, whereas Ralph Singh in *'The Mimic Men'* is an East Indian and belongs to the society he describes. Frankie's objective perspective is essentially having 'otherness'

and though he carries the burden of a guilt—complex, unlike Singh, he has a place to return.

The novella begins with an accidental coming of Frankie—the narrator whose ship is forced to dock on the Caribbean island because of a threatened hurricane. Frankie finds that this is the same island where, once, he had been stationed as a soldier at the American base during the Second World War. As Frankie goes to the island, he observes that though islanders have now got independence with a flag of their own they have become even more unreal than before. Political independence has not released them from their psychological bondage to the colonisers' culture and they continue to live a life of duality and haziness. This is evident in all aspects of life in the surrounding. For instance, the nostalgic expression of the taxi driver for the flag of colonial days is evident. He tells Frankie: **"but I prefer the old union jack. It looks like a real flag. This look like something they make up you know, like foreign money."**[34]

The second part of the novella is a flashback which carries us back to the time when Frankie was a soldier at the American base on the island and had first become acquainted with Henry, Selma, Blackwhite and priest. Henry used to run a brothel in the name of a cultural center. It was here that he had first met Selma whose craze for nice modern things had brought her there. Frankie had bought a house in the street and they had casually started living together. Black white calls himself the principal of a premier commerce college and is also a struggling story writer. His love stories about the lords and ladies relate in no way to the reality of his life. Ma—ho is a Chinese who runs a grocery in the street and has a plan of going back to China. Priest is another contradictory character who first frightens people with his sermons about death and then sells them insurance. Then there is Ma-Ho who joins walking races but always ends up running. Through Frankie's help Ma-Ho finally wins the race but instead of rejoicing he commits suicide. This episode serves as a comment on the negative outcome of the American interference.

The economic boom created by the American presence also has a corrupting effect on the people there. Mr. Lambert, the book binder had a contented life in his small wooden house but his life becomes miserable when he comes to earn twenty dollars a day by hiring out the truck Frankie has stolen from the base. Mr. Lambert's wife starts ill-treating him and even denies entry in his new built house. Selma chides Frankie for his interference in other's lives: **"I don't think I should go around interfering any more in other people's lives. People don't really want what you think they want."** [35] Blackwhite's coloured portrait of Haile Selassie in his front room and the photograph of Chiang Kaishek that Ma-Ho kept concealed between his Chinese calendars were ridiculous affirmations that denied the existence of the island. Black white and Ma-Ho deluded themselves by thinking that they had places to return to when the war ended. However, with the independence the island has a claim to existence and the flag beings the message of its affirmation. Now, there is no escape for people like Blackwhite and Ma-Ho who cherished dreams of another world. Just before independence comes on the island, Ma-Ho dies all of a sudden and his family gets a lot of insurance money. The insularity, the Ma-Ho family had maintained by keeping to themselves, is broken by this death and a rapid cultural disintegration of the family takes place. The adoption of new socialization is evident as:

> "Ma-Ho went, and with him there also went the Chinese emblems in his shop. No longer the neat crocodile left and entered the back door of the shop; and from being people who kept themselves to themselves, who gave the impression of being only temporary residents on the island, always packed for departure, Ma - Ho's family came out. The girls began to ride bicycles. The insurance money was good. The boys began to play cricket on the pavement and Mrs.

> Ma–Ho, who had never spoken a word of English revealed that she could speak the language."[36]

The Third World consciousness evolves in Blackwhite also. He not only abandons the idea of going back but thinks of championing the cause of the native language. He tells Frankie:

> "What we want is our own language. I intend to write in our own language. You know this patios we have. Not English, not French but something we have made up. This is our own you were right. Damn those lords and ladies. Damn Jane Austen. This is ours. This is what we have to work with....."[37]

However, Blackwhite's enthusiasm does not go beyond the statement and ends only with an additional line on the board outside his house - PATIOS TAUGHT HERE. He continues to write in English and his Third World consciousness dies before it has evolved. When the war is over it is only Frankie and his fellow Americans who leave the island.

The final section of the novella brings us back to the present and takes up the story from the point at which the first part had stopped. Frankie sets his foot on the island and is struck by the change that has come over the island and its people. While searching his house, he meets Selma who tells him that she has sold that house and has got a more modern one in a better locality. Selma's new house mimics the modernistic style that has caught on in the island. Even Henry's cultural center is no longer a place where people can walk in casually. It is now a formal joint where people wearing ties are allowed in. Blackwhite now calls himself H.J.B. White and Priest—now Gary Priest land—has become a T.V. personality. But the change is only at the superficial level and there is no inner transformation of the people. Frankie notices that American money and influence still dominate people's taste as the islanders strive to live up to the image that the tourist brochures have created for them. In the name of promoting native culture, the Americans' provide sponsorship only to those local artists who cater to their requirements. Blackwhite has patrons running after him so long us he write, inter-racial love stories but when he tries to be innovative, he is immediately dropped for his crazy ideas. Towards the end of the novel the people, though only momentarily, drop their pretences when the news of hurricane about to destroy this island is spread. At the prospect of being released once and for all from the inauthentic kind of lives that they are forced to live, the islands rejoice with a wave of relief. But this chance also ends in disappointment as the hurricane is averted and some other island is destroyed. Ultimately it is only Frankie and other tourists who leave the island and these expatriates have to accommodate to their trapped predicament.

The mimicry and inferiority of the postcolonial societies in the Third World run like a refrain through all the works of Naipaul and this novella reiterates the same thematic aspect once again. The author holds the colonial past of these societies responsible for their deficiencies and mediocrities. When Blackwhite tells Frankie that had Churchil been born on the island, even he would have ended up importing sewing machines and exporting cocoa because these invalid societies do not have power to mould an individual's potentialities by providing avenues for development. He realises that the unskilled mob of underdeveloped postcolonial world can't be the source of power. Moreover, the mimicry tendency of the postcolonial societies is foretold in the carnival episode of the novel. On the first day of carnival Blackwhite goes dressed in a fantastically braided uniform as 'Mac Arthur promising to return' and on the second evening he poses as Shakespeare. The streets on those two evenings are **"full of great figures—Napolean, Julius Ceaser, Richard the Lionheart—."**[38] Naipaul holds the colonial past of these half - made societies responsible for these deficiencies.

Naipaul's next work '*In a Free State*' (1971) is set in an unnamed African country and it came out in the year in which Naipaul bagged the Man Booker Prize. This novella is akin to *'A Bend in the River'* in its dispersed geographical distribution; the main substance of the work is located in Africa and is complemented and generalised by means of short stories set in Washington and London. As Naipaul has described himself the interpreter of a disordered and fast changing world, a perception of global disorder and displacement is also integral to *'In a Free State.'* Naipaul probes into the paradoxical nature of freedom which instead of liberating the colonial subjects, only makes them the casualties of that freedom. The conversational platitude of the tramp, who is set upon in the first section ironically states the international theme of the work. The novel consists of a prologue and epilogue which enclose two short stories and a novella. Though distinct the three pieces are integrally linked and since priority is given to the examination of freedom in its political, social and psychological dimensions, the fragmented structure does not come as a surprise. The mingling of genres - short story, travel writing and the novella—demonstrates Naipaul's conviction that forms have to be adapted to meet the demands of the material.

Naipaul observes that *'In a Free State'* is a book "**about journeys, unhappy journeys by people switching countries, switching cultures**"[39] and the journey becomes an apt symbol for the world of flux portrayed in the novel. There are exiles, expatriates or tourists coming from different nationalists and all experiencing the throes of rootlessness and homelessness. In the prologue there are people as diverse as Indians, Africans, Americans, Danes, Swedish, Germans, Chinese and Egyptians. The Egyptian Greeks were expelled from Egypt by the invaders but finally Egypt is free and these Egyptians are the casualties of that freedom. Tramp is symbolic figure presenting the predicament of modern man in limbo and his nationality till the end remains unfixed and therefore nationality has lost its meaning at all. He enquires, " **But what is nationality these days? I myself, I think of myself as a citizen of the world.**"[40] Tramps humiliation and beating makes clear that freedom is a hollow word in the eminent chaos that asserts itself and this theme is further explored in the stories that follow and come to conclude with the epilogue. Helen Hayward writes in this connection:

> "The two short stories focus on the experience of protagonists from Southern countries adrift in the metropolitan centre. They portray an anxiety to arrive mingled with a fear of arrival: the threat which attaches to the unfamiliar place; agoraphobia and the dereliction of displaced."[41]

The protagonist of the first story 'One out of Many' is Santosh, an Indian domestic from Bombay but already an American citizen living in Washington. He though a free man and well in life, is unhappy since his life is filled with anxiety and a deeper sense of dereliction. Santosh thinks, **"I wanted the journey to end but I couldn't say I wanted to arrive at Washington."**[42] The unnamed narrator of 'Tell Me Who to Kill' on the way from the west Indies to England, tells him that **"you will never be a freeman again..... I don't want the ship to stop. I don't want to touch land again."**[43] The menace of the adopted country is suggested by the narrator's nostalgia for the ship, once he is on the land: **"It is white and big and safe. It is saying good bye, it is in a hurry to get away and to leave you behind."**[44] This urge to get back on the ship, without knowing any logic for it, is one which Naipaul describes having experienced himself on his first arriving in London. If the journey is a form of imprisonment, so too, is the life of immigrants, as symbolized by Santosh. He is nostalgic for his Bombay life where he had been respected and had enjoyed a certain position. In comparison to the hard life at his village his life in Bombay was privileged one and he had adapted himself to the city. But suddenly problem cropped up when Santosh's employer is posted to Washington in the capacity of a diplomat. He is in a crisis of being out of job but his employer manages to get Santosh's passage sanctioned by the government and he too accompanies his employer to Washington.

In Washington, Santosh faces threats of the new and alien environment and experiences a kind of agoraphobia : **"I was glad I had a place to hide. I had thought of myself as a prisoner. Now I was glad I had so little of Washington to cope with."**[45] Santosh is seen as restricted by his own culturally conditioned perceptions and this tale explores the immigrant's view of the capital of the world, the view of a man from another enclosed culture. It is his involvement with a Hubshi (Hindi for Black) woman that initiates his self-awareness as a man with individual stranded status in new strange world. Here he becomes aware of his own individuality and his perspective changes altogether as he realizes that he can no longer be a part of someone else's presence. He develops a critical eye:

> "Now I found that, without wishing it, I was ceasing to see myself as part of my employer's presence and beginning at the same time to see him as an outsider might see him as perhaps the people who came to dinner in the apartment saw him. I saw that he was a man of my own age, around thirty-five; it astonished me that I hadn't noticed before. I saw that he was plump, in need of exercise, that he moved with short fussy steps.... a man who looked as uneasy in Washington as I felt, who acted as cautiously as I had learned to act."[46]

Along with this self-awareness comes the realisation that he has grown up and his Bombay life to which return is next to impossible could be visualized as the happy times of childhood. This is his new found psychological freedom from his past as well as from his mentor and he now becomes an independent individual in search of a new identity. Deserting his employer he joins Priya an Indian, who runs a restaurant there. Working with Priya makes him feel a man of independent decisions with no overshadowing force any more. But all the freedom thus gained brings loneliness and further fragmentation in his life amidst the wilderness of the modern world. He realizes that freedom and individuality bring responsibilities which he has to face alone and now a deep sense of insecurity haunts him. His status now after running away from his employer, is that of an illegal immigrant and the fear of being discovered constantly nags him. Unable to bear the burden of his freedom, Santosh is on the urge of a breakdown and relapses into his previous psychological state of dependence when, instead of calling Priya by name as he had been doing from the beginning in the stupor of his fear, suddenly addresses her as '*Sahib*'. This reaffirms his inner hollowness and relapse to the master slave relationship. As a result his relationship with Priya undergoes a change. In the end Santosh discloses all his inner ennui, anxiety and secrets to Priya who advises him to marry the Hubshi woman because that is the only way to legalise his stay in Washington. Santosh does accordingly but all this leads to further alienation and disintegration of his life. Resultantly all freedom of Santosh amounts to the mere fulfillment of his physical needs: **"All that my freedom has brought me is the knowledge that I have a face and have a body, that I must feed this body and cloth this body for a certain number of years. Then it will be over."**[47]

The next story 'Tell Me Who to Kill' takes us to the West Indies, the familiar Naipaul territory. The protagonist narrator in this story is an East Indian who is in a more miserable predicament even than that of Santosh. Frustrated with his own life, he nurtures the dream of a better life for his brother Dayo who becomes the obsession of his life. His self-effacement is so complete that he is not given any name and till the end remains Dayo's brothers. The dissociation of the narrator from the life around him imparts him a claustrophobic quantity to the story: **"from the moment of arrival you are like a man in blinkers."**[48]

Christianity is held up as the hallmark of progressiveness and the narrator's role model is his Christian uncle Stephen who is well educated and sends his son to Montreal for higher studies. The narrator also somehow manages to send his brother Dayo to England to study aeronautical engineering and later follows him to London to take care of him. But there he feels that he has lost himself completely and his life has become just a series of journeys to strange places: **"It is always like this now you are always taking trains and buses to strange places you never know what sort of street you are going to find yourself in, what sort of house you will be knocking at."[49]**

All hopes of the narrator are concentrated on his brother but when he discovers that Dayo is simply idling away his time in London, he loses all sense of direction and becomes totally dissociated and lost. He subsequently imprisons himself effectually in work and his psychological disorder is reflected in the envy he feels for tourists in London: **"But these people come for the day; they are happy, they have buses to take them back to their hotels; they have countries to go back to, they have houses. The sadness I feel make my heart seize."[50]**

Dayo's failure makes him feel that his life has shattered to pieces and he loses control over himself. He speaks of his disoriented and alienated predicament. **"I can't see where I am going, I can only wait to see what is going to turn up."** [51] We can't help feeling sympathy for Dayo who becomes deviant and eventually drifts away from his brother and marries an English girl. The narrator is seized with hatred and cries out in utter anguish:

> "O good show me the enemy. Once you find out who the enemy is, you can kill him. But these people here they confuse me. Who hurt me? Who spoil my life? Tell me who to beat back...tell me who to kill."[52]

Naipaul's presentation of the limitations of the immigrants' perceptions raises the question of why it should be that he so often chooses to write from this point of view. Like Biswas in '*A House for Mr. Biswas*' and quite a number of Naipaul's other characters, the narrator of this story also suffers a breakdown. His neurosis is the result of an intense alienation and disillusionment in displaced status in London with which he just could not cope. The narrator of 'Tell Me Who to Kill' is unable to locate his enemy because it is not one person; it is the past of slavery, colonial neglect and a society uneducated and downtrodden for ages. The enemy is the smallness of the islands and the absence of resources. The freedom becomes a state of being aimless and drift, a severance of all ties with the world—a total withdrawal. The narrator who cannot bear to return home after his failure sends back a message that he is dead. He has been reduced to a living corpse.

The title story *'In a Free State'* is set in an English—Indian creation in the African wilderness and picturises a newly independent African country in upheaval and turmoil. The major characters in the story are English and besides some minor African characters there is an American who makes a brief appearance at the background of the novel. There is the tribal war between the tribes of the president and the king. The age old enmity between the different tribes has become intense in the independent era and there is a struggle for power and intrigues are all around. The white people choose to support the president who is in command of the new army and thus stronger than the king.

This disintegration and breakdown of the typical Third World country in the postcolonial turmoil is conveyed to us through the consciousness of Bobby who is an administrative officer in one of the department of central government and lives in the Southern Collectorate, a territory of the king's people. When the novel opens Bobby is in the capital attending a seminar. On community development and it is ironical enough that there are more English participants and few Africans on his drive back Linda, one of the *'compound wives'* joins Bobby and soon he is involved in a conciliating relationship with Linda. They have contradictory views about Africa; Bobby is liberal and protective but Linda racialist. From the scene and incidents we witness, through Bobby and Linda in the course of their long drive the picture that emerges about the state of affairs in this newly independent nation and it is mere chaos. The educated Africans, turn to be ineffectual copies of their white benefactors and their lack of selfhood is reflected in their English-made suits and hair done in the English style. When Linda and Bobby see a large number of Africans in new cloths the former comments on their savage ways: **"Somewhere upon there they've taken off their new clothes and they are dancing naked and holding hands and eating dung."**[53] Even the new officials of Africa, like Sammy Kisenyi, are the product of culturally and intellectually barren background. Summy's fat headedness is reflected in his article on broadcasting read at a conference in which he lifts paragraphs from T.S. Eliot. Champa Rao Mohan writes about this miserable situation after the transfer of power in post colonial Africa as:

> "Naipaul effectively conveys the threat posed by the shift of power which leaves no one safe. Bobby and Linda, being whites are especially vulnerable. The hunt for the king at the background, the unpredictable soldiers and the Africans, whom the colonial only just manages to keep at bay, all serve to underscore the chaos that threatens to break through. The king is finally hunted down brutally and Bobby after a series of humiliations is manhandled by the president's soldiers."[54]

The hunting dogs that have gone wild on being abandoned by their white masters are suggestive image of the prevailing situation in the postcolonial Africa. The dogs become suggestive of the *'Wild Free State'* into which the Africans themselves have fallen after the white masters have left. Bobby no doubt is sincere in saying *"Africa saved my life"* but his interest in Africa is nothing more than self-indulgence. We know that he has come to Africa after recovering from a nervous breakdown because of his homosexual involvements. Bobby's over friendly attitude towards Africans lands him into trouble a number of times. A Zulu youth who is a male prostitute first encourages Bobby and then spits on his face. Two other Africans whom Bobby gives a lift in his car try to bully him and also damage the windscreen of his car at the filling station. Bobby desperately shouts at their wild mindlessness. This incident shows that the Africans are still rustic and wild having no understanding of the borrowed technologies. The interference of the whites in the internal affairs and their developmental programmes are all in reality the policies of the neocolonialism at work in newly independent African country. When the president's soldiers beat Bobby up there is little he can do besides nursing his wounds both physical and psychological. When Bobby gets back to the compound, Luck his house boy, makes a fun of him. The story concludes with Bobby realizing that he would have to leave eventually, but first he would have to dismiss Luke before whom he has been exposed. However, he can think of sacking Luke only because he belongs to the already oppressed king's tribe.

Thus Naipaul's portrayal of Africa in '*In a Free State*' is somehow inauthentic and banal. The Africans are mostly caught in certain fixed attitudes that prove certain preconceived ill notions about this part of the colonized humanity. The mindlessness, mimicry and unpredictable nature of the Africans are projected only to make the point of their inferiority without any sympathetic stance at all. It is disheartening that Naipaul has failed to adopt sympathetic stance with regard to the Africans whose colonial experiences were perhaps the most brutal in the whole history of colonial violation. Naipaul expresses his revulsion for the Africans, that to him are '*Savage*', dirty and smelling and this story seems to complete their dehumanization. The Africans are denied even the moral sense of good and bad and it is insinuated that they are governed by the law of jungle.

Apart from the opinions of Bobby and Linda, there is a third view expressed by the colonel who is in charge of the tourist's resort. The colonel's view is even more damaging one as it presents a completely dehumanized picture of the Africans. The colonel's attitude is clearly expressed in the following conversation between him and Peter, an African youth who works for him:

"What do you think of me, Peter?

'I like you, sir.'

You take me in when I was small. You give me job, you give quarters. You look after my children. He has fourteen. He is living with three of those animals right now. So polished. So nice. So well spoken. You wouldn't believe he doesn't even know how to hold a pen in those hands. You wouldn't believe the filth he comes out of. But you like dirt, don't you Peter? You like going into some black hole to eat filth and dance naked. You will steal and lie to do that, won't you?

'I like the quarters, sir.'

While I live you will stay there. You won't move in here, Peter I don't want you to bank on that. If I die you will starve, Peter. You will go back to bush.'

That is true, sir."[55]

This extract portrays the complete dehumanization that has overtaken Africans who are still '*the Whiteman's burden.* The comment of colonel about Africa in his conversation with Bobby and Linda strengthens this degradation and prevailing hatred in the colonial forces towards their once subjects. **"They say there's good and bad everywhere. There is no good and bad here. They do what they have to do. That is what you have to tell yourself. You can't hate them. You can't even get angry with them. Really angry."**[56] Thus it is insinuated that Africans are governed by the law of jungle and they have no sense or sensibility at all. The colonel views them with a biased eye and in the lens of his own culture. Naipaul is here naked in his whims and inclinations and undoubtedly, he is voicing his own prejudiced opinions through his characters. Otherwise he would have countered it with his own version of the predicament. This is further corroborated by Naipaul's cursory dismissal of African readership in a 1979 interview when he said, **"No, I don't count the African readership and I don't think one should. Africa is land of bush again not a very literary land."**[57]

Naipaul's tone is here Eurocentric and so racial as is evident in the analogy he suggestively draws between the wild dogs and the Africans.

Naipaul's vision falls short of ability to represent the 'subaltern' in the African context. His limitation as a postcolonial intellectual lies in the fact that he makes no attempts to understand the inner working of the African tribal society and its social equations that were totally upset by colonial rule. Landeg White rightly points out: **"... the whole argument is conducted without any African perspective on events. Naipaul's treatment of the people who actually inhabit this country is very rudimentary."**[58]

Naipaul focuses too much on the violence that has been un-leased after independence because the internal fractures or fissures that existed alongside colonialism have now surfaced. Besides *'decolonisation'* is always a violent phenomenon because it is only natural that people who were subjected to centuries of oppression and violence should themselves react with violence. Though delayed this realisation seems to have come to Naipaul later in his career when he defines Nihilism as **"the rage of primitive people coming to themselves and finding that they have been fooled and affronted."**[59]

Naipaul, therefore has been charged of the brutality towards the sensibility of the Third World people because of the insensitive and inhuman analysis of their societies whether it is of West Indies, or India or of Africa. *'In a Free State'* also gives this impression because it presents a total negation of human values in the postcolonial African society. The novel concludes with an entry from Naipaul's journal entitled *'The Circus at Luxor'* which forms the Epilogue. While in the Prologue he remained a detached witness to the bullying of the tramp, in the Epilogue he intervenes to put a stop to the drama of human misery and indignity he witnesses in Luxor. When the miserable desert children are being lured with scraps of food and scared by the ship for entertainment of tourists, Naipaul rushes to the scene and puts step to miserable exhibition of poverty by snatching the whip from the coffee waiter. This indeed is a bold step on the part of Naipaul and human values are sustained above every other consideration.

Tge relentless and detached writer portrays the postcolonial disorders in the form of violence, corruption and disintegration all around against a backdrop of imperfectly apprehended political upheaval and a landscape of neglect and ruin. The ultimate truths of the postcolonial societies have also been portrayed by Naipaul through their inability and inefficiency to digest the freedom from the colonial bondages. The task of nation building after independence becomes a major problem due to social fragmentation and moral degradation. The economic and intellectual bankruptcy, neocolonialism, and fragmentation are the major problems that all the Third World nations are grappling with in the post independence era. Because of the neocolonialism the new found independence ceases to give fruits and meaningfulness to the people of these second rated nations. So in '*The Mimic Men*', '*A Flag on the Island*' and '*In a Free State*' Naipaul has been able to delineate the paradoxical idea of freedom and power in all its nuances. However, whether freedom and power are explored as psychological or political realities they are always experienced as a burden and herein lies the paradox of freedom and power in these novels of Naipaul.

References

1. V.S. Naipaul, ' *The Mimic Men*', (Harmondsworth: Penguin Books, 1983), p. 8.
2. V.S. Naipaul, '*The Overcrowded Barracoon and Other Articles*, (London: Andre Deutsch, 1972. Harmondsworth; Penguin Books, 1976), p. 11.
3. V.S. Naipaul, *The Middle Passage: Impressions of Five Societies – British, French and Dutch in the West Indies and South America* (London: 1962; New York: Vintage books, 1981) p. 29.
4. *Ibid.*, p. 169.

5. Clifford, James. *The Predicament of Culture; Twentieth Century Ethnography, Literature and Art* (Cambridge : Harvard University Press, 1988) p. 15.
6. V.S. Naipaul. '*An Area of Darkness*' ,(London: Penguin Books, 1970) p. 27.
7. *Ibid.,* p. 30.
8. *Ibid.,* p. 11.
9. *Ibid.,* p.189.
10. *Ibid.,* p. 27.
11. *Ibid.,* p. 246.
12. *Ibid.,* p. 252.
13. *Ibid.,* p. 265.
14. Champa Rao Mohan, *op. cit.,* p. 81.
15. Kavita Nandan,' Exile in the Mimic Men': *V.S. Naipaul : An Anthology of Recent Criticism,* (edit) Purabi Panwar, (Delhi: Pencraft International, 2003). p. 127.
16. V.S. Naipaul, '*The Mimic Men*',(Harmondsworth: Penguin Books 1983), p. 175.
17. *Ibid.,* p.32.
18. K.I. Madhusudan Rao. *op. cit.,* p. 84.
19. William Walsh, V.S. Naipaul (Edinburgh 1973) see quoted in Champa Rao Mohan's; *Post Colonial Situation in the Novels of V.S. Naipaul: op. cit.,* p. 84.
20. *The Mimic Men. op. cit.,* p. 83.
21. *Ibid.,* p. 11.
22. *Ibid.,* p. 18.
23. *Ibid.,* p. 100.
24. *Ibid.,* p. 44.
25. *Ibid.,* p. 44-45.
26. Paul Theroux, *V.S. Naipaul: An Introduction to His Works.* (London: Andre Deutsch, 1972) p. 73.
27. *The Mimic Men, op. cit.,* p. 57.
28. *Ibid.,* p. 80.
29. *Ibid.,* p.81.

30. N. Rama Devi, 'Naipaul's Mimic Men : Order and Form Through Art: *V.S. Naipaul's Critical Essays*. (edit) Mohit K.Ray. *op. cit.* p. 35.
31. *The Mimic Men. op. cit.* p. 8.
32. Champa Rao Mohan, *op. cit.* p. 91.
33. Madhusudan Rao, *Contrary Awareness, op. cit.,* p.43.
34. V.S. Naipaul, *A Flag on the Island;* (London: Andre Deutsch: Penguin Books 1971) p. 132.
35. *Ibid.,* p. 175.
36. *Ibid.,* p. 181.
37. *Ibid.,* p. 150.
38. *Ibid.,* p. 165.
39. Jim Douglas Henry. 'Naipaul Unfinished Entrails; *Listener*. 25 Nov. 1971: p. 721.
40. V.S. Naipaul, *'In a Free State'*. (London: Andre Deutsch: 1971. Harmondsworth: Penguin: 1973), p. 11.
41. Helen Hayward. *"The Enigma of V.S. Naipaul"* (New York: Palgrave Macmillan, 2002) p.188 –189.
42. V.S. Naipaul, *'In a Free State', op. cit.* p. 29.
43. *Ibid.,* p. 85.
44. Idem.
45. *Ibid.,* p. 39.
46. *Ibid.,* p. 41.
47. *Ibid.,* p. 61.
48. *Ibid.,* p. 85.
49. *Ibid.,* p. 86.
50. *Ibid.,* p. 99.
51. *Ibid.,* p. 66.
52. *Ibid.,* p. 107.
53. *Ibid.,* p. 173.
54. Champa Rao Mohan, *op. cit.* p. 106.
55. *'In a Free State, op. cit.,* p. 189.
56. *Ibid.,* p. 193.

57. Robert Boyers and Bharati Mukherjee , *'A Conversation with V.S. Naipaul'* , (Salmagundi, 54; 1981), p. 6.
58. Landeg White, *V.S. Naipaul: A Critical Introduction op. cit.*, p. 200.
59. V.S. Naipaul, *The Return of Eva Paron with the Killings in Trinidad.* (Harmondsworth: Penguin Books, 1981) p. 187.

5

Fluidity of Life and Existential Despair in the Ex-colonies

"Nobody is going anywhere. We're all going to hell, and every man knows this in his bones".[1]

– V.S. Naipaul

Though most of the colonies attained their independence by the second half of the 20th century, the Third World Nations, however, are haunted by the ghost of imperialism as they are replete with diverse problems that are the legacy of the colonialism. In the post-colonial era, these nations are experiencing political instability, economic backwardness, socio-cultural disintegration and are also grapping to attain a self-esteem which is yet beyond their reach. This phase has witnessed uncontrollable turmoil, violence and odd situations in these second-rated countries. In such a chaotic aftermath, the expatriate peoples are in a more gruesome predicament since they are already under the curse of exile and their history and culture have been denigrated .In addition to poverty and deracination these uprooted people suffer from a sense of marginalization, alienation and existential despair.

V.S. Naipaul is undoubtedly a relentlessly truthful novelist of Diaspora and being a twice exiled writer of Indian origin, he situates his novels in both the colonial as well as the postcolonial scenario to record a perspective account of the complexities in these nations. Now the novelist endeavours to analyse the deep rooted maladies, paradox of freedom, fluidity of life and existential despair in ex-colonies with a special reference to the expatriate people who are the worst sufferers. Here, a vivid presentation of the violent turmoil and nightmarish experiences in the Third World Nations is made from the point of view of the expatriates living there. Amidst the chaos of the post-independence situations, Naipaul, who himself is a displaced and exiled writer from Indian community in Trinidad, moves in and out of the consciousness of the protagonists coming from the rootless and derelict groups in alien lands. Actually the unique combination of the circumstances which related Naipaul to three societies—the ancestral India, the native Trinidadian and the English of his adoption and intellectual training have sharpened his vision and he maintains a surgeon-like objectivity while exposing the complexities and mutual corruption of both the colonizers as well as the colonized.

Of course, Naipaul's novels at large depict the complexities of the colonial and postcolonial situations, but '*Guerrillas*'(1975) and '*A Bend in the River*'(1979)are vivid presentations of the violent political turmoil and nightmarish experiences in the Third World Nations from the points of view of the expatriates living in the ex-colonies. Naipaul had spent considerable time traveling in Africa and these novels are based on the African subcontinent and his association with the theme of homelessness continues even here. We observe a steady increase in awareness and intellectual concern of Naipaul about the fluidity of life and existential despair looming large in the half-made societies and individuals of the ex-colonies. Champa Rao Mohan epitomizes these thematic aspects of these novels as:

> "The major Naipaulian themes of identity crisis, displacement, homelessness, marginality and neo-colonialism reach their culmination in these two novels even as Naipaul exposes the Black Power movement of the imaginary Caribbean island in *'Guerrillas'* and probes into the dynamics of race politics in *'A Bend in the River"*.[2]

There is a shift of focus to the postcolonial Third World political scenario and social situation as a whole is described in terms of power politics and the individuals just as political beings. This aspect has already appeared in *'The Mimic Man'* where Ralph Singh's political and social experiences have figured either in a triumph or defeat. But in *'Guerrillas'* and *'A Bend in the River'* politics becomes dominant on all the relations—sexual or emotional to such an extent that they end in misogynist violence and desolate situation. Violence is common in these novels and sexual indulgence is for the purpose of exposing the boredom, ennui, disgust and moral condemnation of the people leading a fluid life of instability. Hanna Wirth Nesher observes: **"Sexuality in Naipaul's fiction is contrary to that literary tradition in which nakedness implies stripping men and women of their cultural and political roles as well."**[3]

Indeed the racial and political identities become so integral parts of the post-imperial world that any intimacy—heterosexual or homosexual—becomes impossible and ends in fruitlessness. This bleak tendency reaches its climax in these two novels full of existential despair. Dagmar Barnouw writes about *'Guerrillas'*:

> "In these fictional texts two narrative strategies serve to underline the issue of responsible—cultural (political) judgement—most clearly, most fearlessly in *Guerrillas*. It is Naipaul's darkest, most uninhibited but also most tightly structured account of postcolonial difficulties and ensuing self-delusions. Yet despite the narrational control, the dangerous moral and political

> uncertainties of life suspended in a post-independence vacuum, appear to be not fully known to the third person narrator. There is only partial guidance for the reader in tracing and unraveling the complex of relations between the groping, floating characters in their often hostile environment on a small barren Caribbean island. Their interaction clearly reflects the danger posed by political conflicts and intrigues....."[4]

The action of '*Guerrillas*' takes place in a draught-ridden Caribbean island and rotates around three major characters–Jimmy, Jane and Roche. Naipaul employs the third person omniscient narrator's perspective and dramatises the degenerate politics of the postcolonial phase as he moves in and out of the consciousness of his characters. The novel highlights the Black Power rising, killing of a black leader, eruption of violence and the crumbling of the government. It is based on an incident in Trinidad itself. In this crises-ridden society of a tropical country, the story centers round a place called Thrush Cross Roche, a people's commune. Adela and Harry are from a West Indian background. Naipaul portrays emptiness of the lives of these characters in a town surrounded by forests all around where guerrillas are supposed to be hiding. Ironically enough, although the novel makes references to guerrillas, none of them really exists. The state of being a guerrilla is a universal predicament: **"When everybody wants to fight his own little war, everybody is a guerrilla."**[5] Naipaul seems to be demystifying the idea of guerrilla revolution—it is all rhetoric. Everybody is busy in one's own salvation. The theme of revolution which haunted Naipaul finds its statement more emphatically here. The novel is based on the real life character of Michael X also known as Abdul Malik, whose story Naipaul has published in *'The Return of Eva Peron with the Killings in Trinidad.'* In fictional account, however, he makes some changes to extend its thematic possibilities by introducing two new characters-Roche, the white liberal and Bryant, a black homosexual youth. In fact, the real power still resides outside the island

and everyone living in it, including Roche and Jane are at the margins of power. Fear dominates the novel to the point that it becomes a negatively exhilarating energy which, like the desolation of the place, wears out the protagonists and makes them vulnerable to irrational decisions.

The dual role of the narrator as an involved witness and omniscient observer makes ample scope to delineate characters with all realities of their fractured psyche and diseased soul. *'Guerrillas'* opens into what sounds like Eliot's *'The Waste Land'* and people who inhabit this waste land are quite in tune with it. They are derelict, morally and intellectually barren as is reflected from the derelict surroundings marked by shacks, rags, corrugated iron roofs, junked vehicles and the scars of draught and bushfires; something that the former anti-aparthied activist Peter Roche senses but does not fully understand. Now a public relation consultant—hired by a wealthy island firm—Sablich, once involved in slave trade, he is involved in one of their socially responsible projects, an agricultural commune for 'difficult' young black men. It is run by black-Chinese Jimmy Leung from an island working class family who was trained in England to be a black leader and came back confused and violently resentful. The government fears him because of his 'English Glamour' while the capitalist firms like the Sablich, that have investments in the island, fear him as a Black Power man who can bring about a revolution in the land. Jimmy knows his potentials only too well: "**They've got to support me.... because, if I fail them, I'm the only man that stands between them and revolution and they know it now, massa. That's why I'm the only man they're afraid of.**"[6] Roche is aware of the highly combustible situation as he is a white liberal who has been tortured in South Africa for his involvement in the anti-racial cause and so is an ideal public relations man for the firm with unsavoury past as a slave trading firm. But his wife Jane has just arrived from London and is fascinated rather than alarmed. Ostensibly working for the benefit of the native mostly poor, mostly black population, whites deliberately embrace the difference and dangers of involvement. Jimmy in Roche's view is, of course, absurd in nearly every way but he somehow gets things done and this intends his firm faith on maintaining a cost effective progressive image. In words of Dagmar Barnouw:

> "In the political reality that Roche and Jimmy have accidentally come to share and that Roche, upto a point understands and Jimmy enacts, there is no good or bad, only an anarchic struggle that seems unstoppable to Roche. Jane has never been in real danger and her selective, distorting view of the situation reinforces her dangerous illusion that she will always have the opinion of escape."[7]

Naipaul continues his exploration of the theme of the postcolonial predicament of newly decolonized countries; the involvement of the whites of the island comes in for criticism. The white people face a peculiar situation. They are no more rulers; they are no more wanted; they come only for sexual excitement, seeking freedom; their existence has lost all the former glamour. The political situation is rendered not directly but obliquely through the psychological reflex of individuals drawn into the vortex of revolution. Jimmy calls the commune "Thrushcross Grange" and leads the slum youths to bring about a revolution based on land. The intricately worked out characters establish an association with English literary tradition as well as in their subversion and ironical re-reading radiate complex ambiance of this new novel of the Third World. Roche knows that most people on the land accept strange, unsettling and dangerous behaviour engaging in their own little wars, uniting momentarily when things really get out of hand in view of whoever has the power at that moment. It does not take long for Jane to realize that Roche's position in the island is no better than that of a refugee. Her disillusionment with her white lover takes her to Jimmy but the relationship takes off on a wrong footing with Jane dominating over Jimmy on their first sexual encounter and incurring his hatred. In one scene a shocked Roche is watching Jane flinging her empty tampon box against the wall. They have moved apart and he sees that distance expressed on the changing sense of her body: **"it was as though she didn't belong to her body, as though there was some spirit within her that was at odds with the body whom she yet cherished and whose needs she thought to satisfy."**[8] This conflict makes her more vulnerable to Jimmy's physical aggression but if Roche has a sense of being in danger, he does not act on it. Surely an announcement of her love affair with Jimmy is defiantly self-assertive. Likewise, Roche's idea about Jane also undergoes a change after she joins him at the Ridge because what London has marked, the Ridge now too late, has made plain. When he had first met her in London he had considered her to be coherent person with a point of view. But after coming close Roche now finds a person suffering from the psychological vacuum, incoherent thought process and loss of memory and therefore is full of contradictions. Roche has been profoundly irritated by her simple dismissal of the difficulties of the post-colonial requirements for a reconstruction at the national as well as individual level. Dagmar Barnouw writes on this predicament of women:

> "Naipaul's women characters are often sexually self-absorbed and controlling, indicating his, perhaps in some way, flawed view of women, but the writer has put this personal limitation to good use."[9]

In the meanwhile the situation in the island becomes explosive when Stephen, one of the inmates of the commune, is killed by the police. Jimmy picks up a big procession showing the dead body around the town and violence breaks out. Mob becomes riotous and police finds itself unable to control the violent uprising. In the picaroon society everyone is a guerrilla-privateer-fighting for his or her own little cause. People wait for the events to give shape to their amorphous lives. However, normalcy returns when the American planes arrive to take control of the situation. When the mob rejects Jimmy's leadership, he gets a rude shock and realizes that he is a finished man.

On the other hand Jane and Roche have become disoriented and decentered human beings in their venture to such a cause and purpose in their deficient world. Being disenchanted and disappointed, they both decide to leave the island. Jane goes to meet Jimmy before going away and he, frustrated as he is, subjects her to an indirect insult. He sodomises her and then offers her to his abused crazy, young, black lover Bryant who kills her. Roche helps Jimmy to erase all evidence about Jane's presence in the island and escape to London. However, the narrator's approach towards the male characters is essentially sympathetic and they are presented as victims of their circumstances. The dual role of the narrator as an 'involved witness and omniscient observer' provides Naipaul ample scope and full freedom to delineate his characters in a vivid and subtle manner. Champa Rao Mohan observes:

> "Most of the characters are made available to us directly as the narrator enters their consciousness and exposes them. There is an ironic contrast between what the characters think and feel and what they say and do. In addition to the peep we get into the psyche of the characters, they are subject to further assessment through their perceptions about one another."[10]

This is true of all including the physically repulsive Bryant as well as murderous Jimmy who emerge as equally pathetic figures. Bryant, in spite of his threatening appearance, is sensitive enough to cry when he realizes the potentials that have gone wasted in him:

> "Watching the film, he began to grieve for what was denied him: that future in which he became what he truly was, not a man with a gun, a big profession or big talk but himself, and as himself was loved and readmitted to the house and to the people in the

house. He began to sob....."[11]

Jane initially thinks of Roche as a doer and the island as the setting for his action. But this image nurtured in her mind is shattered when on coming to the island she perceives that he was a man who didn't have a place to go back to; he was someone for whom room had been made. Likewise, for Jimmy too, all the aura of power that surrounds Bryant, turns out to be a mere play thing in the hands of the radical groups that patronize him. This reality becomes apparent in Jimmy's correspondence with a man called Roy and it lays bare his inner feeling of insecurity and vulnerability. Incidentally, the letter is written before the riots actually break out:

> "The situation is desperate Roy, the people here have been betrayed too often, it's always a case of black faces white masks, you don't know who your enemy is, the enemy infiltrates your ranks all the time. Mass Mister Roche he's very importunate in his inquiries about one of the boys they sent here, Stephen a little gang leader from the city, a big coup for them, they thought he was going to take over from me..... But the situation is getting desperate now, in the still of the night I lose my courage, I feel it's a losing battle, they're sending other agents, I don't know how to cope."[12]

In case of Jane, however, we find a total lack of sympathy for this character on Naipaul's part. Even the description of the murder scene is done in a passionless, clinical manner.

Jimmy, who professes to be the leader of the black power movement in the island, is no more genuine and is meant as a foil to expose the farce and futility of the movement. Life is in utter suspension when the riots broke out and Jimmy, as a rejected leader, is not in a position to control it. There is a futility of life all around and in utter confusion that breaks loose even the police "**don't know who they're**

fighting or who they fighting for."[13] In fact, everyone seems to be a guerrilla and the guerrillas we meet—Roche, Jane, Jimmy and the boys at the commune are derelicts who have no sense of purpose in life and only just carry on. Jimmy's half-caste status renders his position as the leader extremely ironical and inefficient. As Meredith, the political drop out tells Roche while interviewing him that Jimmy, being half-Chinese, could not have been in tune with the aspirations of black people. Jimmy is incapable of making distinction between the two because he is a cultural schizophrenic. He is the archetypal Naipaulian mimic man and this is evident in the interior arrangement of his home which mimics English middle class suburbia to such an extent that Jane on her first visit cries out: **"But it is like being in England."**[14] Moreover, the name of his commune "Thrushcross Grange" is borrowed from Bronte's novel *'Wuthering Heights'* and there is identification of Jimmy with Healthcliff and this involves a number of ironies. It emphasizes Jimmy's desire to be accepted by the white world and by white English women in particular. The characters in *'Guerrillas'* are both at a distance from *'Wuthering Heights'* and yet do radiate a close affinity to them. The intricately worked out allusions both establish an association with English literary tradition as well as in their subversion and ironical re-reading radiate the complex ambiance of this new novel of the Third World. If the leadership is such, the followings can also be no better and so least authentic. Naipaul's apocalyptic vision offers an extremely dismal view of the post-imperial world where life is instable and fluid and things have fallen apart with no hope of any fresh beginning. The world in *'Guerrillas'* is on the brink of extinction and this is evident in the Ridge, the city and the commune all of which are described in terms of decay and " **no one will make afresh start or do anything new."**[15] Down in the city the society has already collapsed and what remains is "**a community without rules.**" [16] This fluidity of life and impermanence of the world threatens to spread up and is reinforced through Jimmy's realization that: **"There are no more mansions. I suppose, like everyone**

else, I fooled myself that there was a mansion waiting somewhere for me."[17] The dominating and intense mood of the novel is one of the existential despair, fluidity of life, and utter pessimism. As Sashi Karma observes: "**It is similar to existential absurdity: of anguish at living in an unrelated meaningless world; in a void.**"[18] To Naipaul the post-imperial world has no center to hold. Both the left out colonizers as well as the colonized people are at the margins of power but each group identifies the center with the other.

Obviously, the condition of the half-made society in this second-rated country is miserable as the flux of post-colonial upheaval has made disintegration, deracination and meaninglessness the dominant characterstics of the life of the people here. Their search for power also meets with failure just like their quest for identity and freedom. For Jimmy the quest ends in a fiasco and for Jane it proves to be fatal. Roche only just manages to escape from the island and saves himself. Finally, it is Meredith, the colonial politician who becomes the minister but we can not derive any positive meaning out of it. This only reiterates the unpredictable and chaotic nature of politics in the Third World.

'A Bend in the River', one of the most powerful novels of Naipaul, is yet another example of the unpredictability and chaos in the deteriorating post-imperial Third World. The novel is set in an unnamed African country undergoing political turmoil and so portrays the nightmarish experiences of the expatriates living there. Naipaul had spent considerable time traveling in Africa and this novel is yet another example of travel writing transmuted into fiction. Here, Naipaul employs the third person omniscient narrator's perspective to dramatise the extremely vulnerable position of the expatriates, especially Indians. Salim, who has a small business, travels a long way to the heart of the continent accompanied by Metty, son of one of the family's slave and becomes a trader in this town on the bend of the river. Amidst the chaos of the post-independence turmoil the novelist moves in and out of the consciousness of the

protagonist Salim—an East Indian Muslim whose group of community and racial people are settled in this continent for generations but they are still rootless derelicts. By setting the novel in the wider context of Africa, Naipaul has broadened the perspective of the themes he has developed here-to-fore. However, the landscape with the river, the rapids, the steamer service, the events and the close modeling of the Big Man's character on Mobutu, make it obvious that the unnamed country is non other than Congo or Zaire. The Europeans had come there in search of gold and silver and have left the town now after the end of the colonial rule. However, they have left some statues built in their honour here. Zabeth is a small merchant, a magician and a sorceress of a sort. Ferdinand, her son who is of mixed tribal heritage, is a boarder at school; Mahesh and Shobha, an Indian couple have a gaudy flat. Father Huisman is a benevolent Christian and a friend of Africa, though he soon comes to be regarded as an enemy. However, he has faith in the future of Africa. The President, an African, is a modernizer who has rediscovered the African soul. Salim and Yvetta have an affair but she also has a good time with Inder and Raymond. It is depicted as a place in postcolonial Africa where civilized values confront their savage negation; an arena for the regressive display of savage instincts in which the immigrants discover their identity due to the obliteration of their past. The expatriates—heterogeneous peoples who occupy a small patch of land in the town at the bend of the rive—are a few Bulgarians, some Greeks, Italians and Indians living **"a stripped Robinson Crusoe kind of existence".**[19] They are in an extremely miserable predicament since the violence and chaos have fostered a fear-psychosis of complete dissolution and loss in exile. The river—the timeless river—is a silent witness to their agonies and thus shares the making and unmaking of the civilization on the postcolonial relics here.

As Naipaul deals with the themes of slavery, violence and paradox of freedom and power, he questions many assumptions of the Third World; the racial and political tension, the disorder and destruction and above all the disintegration and alienation of man from society and the landscape. The prevailing contradictions, contemporary events and complexities of this newly independent nation are visualized through Salim who attributes his predicament of nowhereness to the uprooted and homeless existence of his people. So homelessness which was a personal condition of Naipaul, continues to be associated here also and derelict expatriates are unnerved by their existential anguish and despair. With the passage of time these people have lost their historical identity and have fallen adrift on this savaged land. Even Inder, Salim's friend from the Hindu community, realizes this anomaly of their floating existence. He tells Salim: **"We're washed up here, you know. To be in Africa you have to be strong. We're not strong. We don't even have a flag."**[20]

The protagonist is restless and anxious to search some authentic identity and this quest is intensified by the effects of financial instability and conflicts all around. Obviously, overwhelmed with an existential despair, Salim seems to renounce his ties with his family at coastal Africa and he moves on a daring journey towards this town to evolve some substitute identity in limbo. Such contradictions of Africa are focused through Salim's stream of consciousness and he attributes his pessimism and insecurity to the loss of his roots. The disorder and chaos in the surrounding has caused an inner fragmentation and an undefineable malaise to him. Actually the protagonist seems to share the restlessness and audacity of Naipaul when he speaks of this realization and resolution as:

> "To stay with my community, to pretend that I had simply to travel along with them, was to be taken with them to destruction. I could be master of my fate only if I stood alone. One tide of history—forgotten by us, living only in books by Europeans that I was yet to read—had brought us here. We had lived our lives in our way, done what we had to do, worshipped God and obeyed his commandments. Now—to echo Inder's words—another tide of history was coming to wash us away."[21]

So Salim breaks away from his family to take over a store in the town at the bend of river amidst the strange assortments there. But it is ironical that Salim again finds himself trapped in a more miserable situation here than his life at the coast from which he had sought an escape. Actually, in spite of the evacuation and withdrawal of the imperial powers, the condition here has deteriorated due to the violent conflicts of the new forces grappling for the reign of the land. The second rebellion as well as the liberation army that proclaims itself in the later part of the novel, exhibits the nihilistic impulses that seek to destroy everything that is not African. Naipaul describes this African nihilism as the rage of the primitive men coming to themselves and finding that they have been cheated, fooled and affronted. So the town at the bend is destroyed and the ruins speak of "**the depth of that African rage, the wish to destroy, regardless of consequences.**"[22] In the violence that has swept during the second rebellion, the expatriates are extremely vulnerable because the tribal forces have destroyed the town since, "**it is a remainder of the intruders who had ruled in it and from it.**"[23] Salim is frightened on seeing this destruction but now it is also not possible for him to return to the coast because, due to the uprisings, in the meanwhile, his family members have also scattered.

Naipaul picturises the morbid consciousness of the protagonist through his weird relations with different people he encounters at the town. Broadly speaking, there are two sets of characters that have a close interaction with Salim; Metty, Zabeth, her son Ferdinand and Father Huisman represent the African history and civilization; and the other set consists of the East Indians—Nazruddin, Mahesh, his wife Shobha and Inder who are radically his own and in their exile experiencing almost the same ordeal in this flux and chaos. These Indians try to convince Salim that they are nothing more than derelicts and only option before them is to face their lives stoically. In the gruesome predicament Nazruddin exhorts him to learn business tactics; Mahesh explains the casualness of the sexual relationships and Inder initiates him to the philosophy of learning to trample the past since the sour need of the time is to survive without any further illusionary interpretation or consolation. Inder tells Salim the harsh reality of their existence as **"the world is in movement and the past can only cause pain."**[24]

Through Salim's consciousness, Naipaul presents the complex reality of modern Zaire and places great emphasis on slavery and slave trading history. It exhibits the relationship of master to slave as an example of dependency that swallows the identity of individuals in subordination. Though indentured during the imperial rule by their colonial masters, these Asians are drifting like ragged Africans utterly abject in the postcolonial upheaval and chaos. This sharing of the mixed history and existence in Africa increases Salim's agony since even the ancestral past of his community is now a close ended darkness. He observes:

> "Africa was my home, had been the home of my family for centuries. But we came from the east coast and that made no difference. The coast was not truly African. It was an Arab-Indian-Persian-Portuguese place, and we who lived there were really people of the Indian Ocean. True Africa was at our back. Many miles of scrub or desert separated us from the up-country people; we looked East to the lands which we traded—Arabia, India, Persia. These were also the lands of our ancestors. But we could no longer say that we were Arabian or Indian or Persian; when we compared ourselves with these people, we felt like people of Africa."[25]

Salim's pessimism and existential despair, like that of Naipaul himself, is to some extent, temperamental but it is intensified by the negative effects of the rapid political changes and violence all around him. The homelessness and nowhereness of the protagonist reflects the predicament of the fluid life equally experienced by the novelist himself who could never find his final home after he left his family fold once. Meditating on such a morbid situation Salim speaks:

> "Nothing stands still. Everything changes. I will inherit no house and no house that I built will now pass to my children. That way of life has gone. I have lost my twenties, and what I have been looking for since I left home hasn't come to me. I have only been waiting. I will wait for the rest of my life....
>
> Later, I woke up to the solitude of my bedroom, in the unfriendly world. I felt all the child's headache at being in a strange place....I was homesick, had been homesick for months. Home was something in my head. It was something I had lost. And in that I was like the ragged Africans who were so abject in the town we serviced."[26]

In this perspective, the Europeans have been better equipped to deal with the aftermath of the colonial Africa because they were able to cope with the changing situation and to fight or to meet the Africans halfway. On the other hand Indians, rather all Asians continue to live blindly as they had always done.

In the town at the bend of the river Salim comes in contact with three Indian families but develops a special affinity with Mahesh and his wife Shobha. So far as Africans are concerned, the rebels have destroyed the town at independence only to express their long pent up anger against the rule of the high-handed European power. Coming out of the bush, having suffered so much and brought so much suffering on them these people seem half-crazed to Salim. Feeble and hungry they need the town but like a natural force their rage can not be assuaged by reasonable talk or action. In Naipaul's Africa the situation is further complicated by this new destructive force—the African nihilism, which Naipaul describes as "**the rage of primitive men coming to themselves and finding that they have been fooled and**

affronted."[27] The Liberation Army seeks to overthrow the Bigman's regime and revive the old ways and so the war has started up again.

The only Africans Salim knows closely and comes in direct contact with are Zabeth—his customer and her son Ferdinand whose guardianship she has entrusted to him. Otherwise he feels insecure in coming close to Africans because he knows from experience that deeper than all other fears is the terror of strange Africans spreading violence. The rumour of the President's soldiers running away with guns indicates that there is an imminent uprising in the town. Father Huisman, the Lycee's Bulgarian headmaster, has deep interest in African cultural artifacts and therefore makes expeditions to the interior villages to collect African masks and carvings. He observes the destruction of the town as an inevitable setback, as the things that happen when the course of history was being altered. Though he has love for Africa and Africans, he has a greater reverence for everything connected with European colonization. He sees true Africa as '**dying or about to die**'[28] and as its last lucky witness seeks to collect and preserve its cultural remains. As the ruins testify, there can be no mingling of the people of binary—the colonizers and the colonized and any attempt to do so would only end in utter destruction. Father Huisman's killing is a further proof of this fact. He meets his gruesome death when he goes on one of his trips to the interiors and this happens just after the army quells another tribal uprising. He meets his gruesome end when he goes on one of his trips to the interior Africa.

To all the expatriates, Father Huisman's killing is a sort of warning that they must not forget that they are in Africa and the unruffled life in the town indicates that such killings create no sense of loss or pain to the people there. The postcolonial scenario in Africa, as it is in Trinidad is a chaotic one. There are diverse groups and parties and there is violence; a mini civil war. Naipaul's vision of the independent Africa of the times is pessimistic and symbolic. It is an apocalyptic vision; a gruesome one. Living in the midst of fierce fighting all around, especially fighting initiated by the liberation army, Metty observes: "**They're going to kill everybody who can read and write 'everybody whoever put on a jacket and a tie, everybody who is a jacket de boy....They're going to kill and kill. They say it is the only way to go back to the beginning before it's too late.**"[29] The prediction of Father Huisman that there will always be a settlement at the bend of the river comes true and the town begins to grow under the regime of the Big Man. With a vision of a new African consciousness, the Big Man tries to modernize the old Africa and introduces Big burger franchise:

> "All kinds of projects were started. Various government departments came to life again, and the new town at last became a place that could be made to work. We already had the steamer service; now the aircraft was recommissioned and extended, to take the jets from the capital (and to fly in soldiers). We even began to get a new telephone system. It was far too elaborate for our needs, but it was what the Big Man in the capital wanted for us."[30]

The signs of modernization and westernization appear in the stupendous projects at the 'State Domain' where the new grandeur buildings, which include a polytechnic college, a modern farm and residences for new intellectual class, tell the story of new developments. Being built on the ruins of it is the Big man's miracle carrying the message that "**Under the rule of our new president miracle had occurred. Africans had become modern men who built in concrete and glass and set in cushioned chairs covered in imitation velvet.**"[31] But the image of new Africa is unreal and modernization is another form of mimicry; the old Africa is always visible beneath the surface décor of the new. The people do not identify themselves with this new African consciousness and for them the mystery and peace lie in the bush. Naipaul is skeptical about this unbridled freedom and fast pace modernization in Africa and opines that the natives have to pay their price for these developments. Moreover, he draws our attention to the undercurrent where the socialism of the President is just a mask for the personal dictatorship. On the one side the President is trying to westernize his country, on the other he encourages the cult figure of the African Chief. Here Naipaul is obviously supporting the white colonial belief that the natives of the ex-colonies can not be trusted to govern themselves.

It is equally ironical that modern Africa is rather more danger prone than the colonial times and so it can't be a home for the people like Zabeth and even Ferdinand who experiences the anxieties of the transitional world. Ferdinand joins the Domain on a government scholarship after finishing his education at Lycee. While Salim knows that the shoddy grandeur is a hoax, he can not help envying Ferdinand for having admittance into the world of the Domain. The exiled narrator sadly reflects that fluidity of life is his destiny since neither the town nor the Domain can provide him with a home. After Ferdinand has left the Domain and it is discovered that Metty has a family somewhere in the town, the protagonist feels betrayed and defrauded in his loneliness in the town. His own alienation makes him reflect on the desolation of the world and on the fluidity of the exiled life.

The novel presents a conjuring up of an Indian culture in exile in Africa where Mahesh, Inder and Nazruddin have somehow learnt the art of equipping themselves to cope up with the fluid conditions of their lives and have somehow yielded to this irrecoverable loss and have started taking life casually. Salim, the narrator, is unable to break away from the links of his past and on realizing that his original identity is melting, he is also on a persistent quest to authenticate his own existence. It is this search for identity that he migrates to the town and vainly hopes to share the progress and glamour brought there at the behest of the Europeans. In this perspective also the left-over Europeans are better equipped than the Indians to deal with the Africans because they know how to adjust with the changing situations and how to prove their indispensability in the process of modernization of their nation. Though Salim establishes close affinity with an African lady Zabeth who entrusts to him the guardianship of her son Fedinand, yet he is haunted by a fear-psychosis of death and loss because he knows from experience that the fatal threat on the land is from the Africans and obviously the East Indian expatriates are the most vulnerable victims.

Under the regime of the Big Man, who tries to modernize his country with a vision of a new African consciousness, the town also begins to grow and various new projects are started there. The most stupendous project, however, is the 'State Domain' where the signs of westernization appear in the new grandiose buildings. All this carries Big Man's message that under the new rule the new things have occurred to make Africa modern, but this image is unreal; the old Africa is always visible beneath the surface décor of the new one. Naipaul is skeptical about this new found freedom and progress of Africa and dissents that even natives have to pay for it. He draws our attention to the paradox of freedom and to the undercurrent where the socialism of the President is just a mask for disguising his personal dictatorship. It is ironical that on the one side the Big Man is westernizing his country ,but on the other he encourages the cult figure of the African Chief. Here Naipaul seems to support the white colonial belief that the natives of the ex-colonies are incompetent and savage and still they can't be trusted to govern themselves.

As the Africans are outrageous to eliminate all that is not African, the expatriates are in the grip of terror and uncertainty. The incident of the killing of Father Huisman, in spite of his love and craze for African cultural artifacts, is sufficient to prove that there can't be any harmonious absorption of the immigrants on this land....be they Asians or Europeans and any attempt to this effect would end up in self-destruction. The brutal killing of Father Huisman comes as a warning to all the immigrants that they are in Africa—

the land that can never realize that miserable marginalization and desolation is the destiny of all the people exiled on this land of bush. He sadly reflects that neither the town nor the Domain provides him any sense of belongingness and a flux existence has become his destiny for ever. In utter despair he waits for some transformation like a prisoner as he observes: "**I was waiting for some illumination to come to me, to guide me to the good place and the life I was still waiting for.**"[32]

At this critical juncture Inder re-enters Salim's life by coming to the town as a government guest at the Domain. It is through Inder that Salim meets the President's 'Whiteman'—Raymond and his wife Yvette. Though for a very short period Salim feels rejuvenated as the vacuum of his life is filled with an affair that develops between him and Yvette. In spite of knowing that the shoddy grandeur is merely a hoax, he is dazzled with the glamorous life of the idealized Europe in the Domain without any human promises at all. But, in the due course, Salim discovers the malaise of despair and non-entity lurking from behind the seeming glamour of Raymond and Yvette also. During their intimate sexual encounters when Yvette shares her fears and frustrations in the uncertain life at the Domain of Big Man, Salim is shocked to learn that every immigrant is defrauded and doomed to defraud all those who come close to him or her. The external chaos and uncertainty put a strain on Salim and Yvette's sexual relation and it ends only in disgust and aversion. Actually, in his sexual encounters with this white woman Salim's search was not for indulgence but for some deep rooted sense of belongingness in which he fails. Whereas in '*Guerrillas*' the white woman is sexually abused and murdered, in this novel the humiliation of the white woman expresses Naipaul's agnostic attitude towards sex if it is without any sense of self-esteem. In a predicament of alienation, Salim observes: "**We stood for ourselves. We all had to survive. Because we felt our lives to be fluid, we all felt isolated and we no longer felt accountable to anyone**

or anything."[33] Actually Yvette, Raymond, Mahesh, Salim, Inder are all outsiders floating in void without any definite identity or destination. The disorganized and disordered society of the town does not provide them any fulfillment at all. Unlike Mahesh, Salim does not allow himself to become nothing and less than nothing. Being frustrated from all sides, he tries to derive some solace and strength by turning to his communal roots and so becomes engaged with Nazruddin's daughter Kareisha to whom he had given his self-proclaimed commitment long ago. He reaches London to see Nazruddin and to get relief from the agonies of oblivious existence in Africa. But here also his experiences darken his morbidity because he finds the city as something shrunken, mean and forbidding. Moreover, his humiliation at an Indian office by the diplomats of his own ancestral race shatters all his romantic illusions and sentimental attachments with his ancestral roots. In the loneliness and seclusion of the hotel room his agonies are multiplied as he is confirmed of his nowhereness and dereliction at large. The Indian diplomat's words pierce him very deep and he feels himself only a forlorn and out-cast being. The diplomat scolds him **"You people have been living the good life in Africa. Now that things have got a little rough you want to run back But you must throw in your lot with the local people."**[34] Salim gets his inner-self fractured and mutilated and all his expectations with his own ancestral land are shattered to pieces. In the solitude of the hotel room his old anxieties get multiplied by his new ones and he is nothing more than a haunted being.

Out of anguish Salim again returns to the African town with a wish to run his shop but he is traumatized to know that even it has been taken over by the state under the new policy of radicalization. Citizen Theotime is the state trustee-in-charge of the shop and Salim has no other right except becoming simply its manager. Now, he is reduced to a derelict man of no essence at all since his business, his house, his money, his friends and even his servants are of no account to him anymore. The fresh outbreak of violence in the unregulated town aggravates his despair and disgust. Salim's last attempt to salvage some of his losses through clandestine trading in ivory results in his imprisonment. Fortunately, his life is saved by Ferdinand who turns out to be the new commissioner and arranges for Salim's escape from the turbulent place. Ferdinand's departing words to Salim encapsulate Naipaul's vision of the Third World as:

> "You mustn't think it's bad just for you. It's bad for everybody. That's the terrible thing. It's bad for prosper, bad for the man they gave your shop to, bad for everybody. Nobody is going anywhere. We're all going to hell, and everyman knows this in his bones. We are being killed. Nothing has any meaning. That is why everything is so fanatic. Everyone wants to make his money and run away. But where? That is what is driving people mad..... But there is no place to go.....nowhere is safe now."[35]

The ending of *'A Bend in the River'* is also bleak as there is a note of offended superiority and disgust. Salim has developed a capability to absorb the external changes into his consciousness. Through Salim and Inder's consciousness Naipaul portrays the oddities and complexities prevailing in the African ex-colonies. Like a war reporter the novelist effectively reports the tragic vision of the mutilation and fragmentation of the sensibilities of the people amidst the violence and disorder. The political turmoil serves as a backdrop to the tragic drama of their suffering. Nevertheless, Salim, the protagonist emerges as a tragic hero who has earned a capacity to register shame and to reflect on his failures.

The novel reiterates the fact that Naipaul has made an uncompromising commitment to truth as his critical and observant eyes lay bare the malaise of the soul and psyche of the expatriates in the alien environment. He is relentless in exposing how desperately they attempt to seize upon the fluidity of life with a wish to attain some authentic identity and meaningful existence. Through the rich array of characters Naipaul delineates the gruesome realities in this African nation and the worst affected victims of this post-imperial turmoil are the expatriates who have been reduced to non-entity in exile. Their historical identity has already been denigrated and they are in the predicament of *'no land men'*.

It is equally obvious that Naipaul has noticed that the political independence could offer little hope of change to the Third World societies that have been badly maimed and the imperialistic powers continue to retain their indirect hold on the former colonies through newer and more camouflaged methods of new-colonialism. The Big Man, though not physically present, looms large as a paradigm of dictatorship in the big photographs put up everywhere. He is atypical example of the 'Blackman' who has assumed all the lies of the 'Whiteman' in the postcolonial power politics in the Third World nations.

Moreover, through the depiction of the protagonist's journey to London Naipaul puts forward a new dimension of the theme that violence, displacement, alienation and loss of identity are a universal phenomenon in the post-second World War scenario and one must learn to survive with this ultimate truth. Salim also arrives at this wisdom but only after experiencing the ordeal through the hard ways of the world and therefore his struggle gives a positive message to the modern man. Lilian Feder in his book *'Naipaul's Truth'* has rightly remarked:

> "This is not, as it has often been judged, a pessimistic novel. There is tragic optimism in this individual struggle to create a self-pitched niche againgst continents whose past and present history calculated to negate it."[36]

Therefore, in spite of the pessimistic vision in the novel, the human concern makes it much more powerful one compared to *'Guerrillas'*. The difference between the protagonists of the two novels lies in the fact that whereas

Jimmy is unable to break away from the colonial state of dependence, Salim, due to his acquired wisdom of self-appraisal, knows where exactly he stands and this insight makes him take the positive step of rejoining the world. His faith in self becomes the testament of his new philosophy expressed in the opening line of the novel as: **"The world is what it is; men who are nothing, who allow themselves to be nothing have no place in it."**[37] Thus whereas '*Guerrillas*' ends in utter dismay, in '*A Bend in the River*' Naipaul offers a wisdom and hope for the exiled expatriates to mitigate their agonies amidst the fluidity of life and existential despair in limbo.

There is also the ambiance of a subtle parallelism between Salim and Virgil's Aeneas. Karl Miller suggests a correspondence between Salim's adventures and those of Aeneas:

> "Virgil's Aeneas leaves a burning Troy to go on to his adventures, effect his betrayal and arrive at the Tiber, where an empire is to rise. Salim is an Aeneas who makes it to London, where those of his blood are founding a way of life; and he has his Dido both in Yvette and in Metty. Perhaps this much can be said without suggesting that the book is an epic for Kenya Asians, which tells of a people threatened by nobodies, nothings and managing to survive."[38]

All these allusions help to build an atmosphere of a rich and complex epic. '*A Bend in the River*' is an epic of Africa; of its journey in the post-colonial world. The journey of Africa continues and the end of the novel suggests this journey:

> "At the time what we saw was the steamer, searchlight, playing on the river bank, playing on the passengers barge that had snapped loose and was drifting in an angle through the water hyacinths at the edge of the river..... The searchlight, while it was on, had shown thousands, white in the white light."[39]

One more point that needs to be mentioned about '*A*

Bend in the River' is the noticeable change in Naipaul's treatment of Africa and African characters. Not only is he more sympathetic but here is a sincere attempt on his part to analyse and arrive at an understanding of the problems that have gripped the post-independent Africa. However, due to internal fractures in the post-colonial Third World societies, the native liberation movements fail to play a positive role in the formation of an authentic Third World consciousness. In lack of any collective solution Naipaul seems to suggest that the solution is to be strived and obtained at individual level through self-decolonization—that is by overcoming the colonial fear-psychosis and deep-rooted complex of inferiority and self-hatred in the mentality of the people of the ex-colonies. Here, Naipaul seems sympathetic to the African impulse to destroy all the physical reminders of the European presence on their land. Simultaneously, the author makes it clear that destruction of the surface features is not sufficient, the whole attitude and vision must experience the ordeal and evolution of a new decolonized perception. However, *'A Bend in the River'* concludes with Naipaul's failure to arrive at any positive conclusion about Africa which, according to him, is a land of bush.

References

1. V.S. Naipaul, *A Bend in the River, op. cit.,* p. 320.
2. Champa Rao Mohan, *op. cit.,* p. 119.
3. Hanna Wirth Nesher, 'The Curse of Marginality: Colonialism in Naipaul's Guerrillas;' *Modern Fiction Studies.* 30.3 (1984), p. 544.
4. Dagmar Barnouw, 'Other Lives Novels'; *Naipaul's Strangers,*(Bloomington and Indianapolis: Indian University Press, 2003), p. 33.
5. V.S. Naipaul, *Guerrillas,* (London: Andre Deutsch,1975, Harmondsworth: Penguin Books, 1976), p. 87.
6. *Ibid.,* p. 27.
7. Dagmar Barnouw, *op. cit.,* p. 35.

8. V. S. Naipaul, *Guerrillas, op. cit.,* p. 123.
9. Dagmar Barnouw, *op. cit.,* p. 36.
10. Champa Rao Mohan, *op. cit.,* p. 121.
11. V.S.Naipaul, *Guerrillas, op. cit.,* p. 37.
12. *Ibid.,* p. 86.
13. *Ibid.,* p. 185.
14. *Ibid.,* p. 24.
15. *Ibid.,* p. 149.
16. *Ibid.,* p. 103.
17. *Ibid.,* p. 87.
18. Shashi Karma, *The Novels of V.S. Naipaul.*(New Delhi: Prestige, 1990), p. 37.
19. V.S. Naipaul, *A Bend in the River, op. cit.,* p. 28.
20. *Ibid.,* p. 21.
21. *Ibid.,* p. 22.
22. *Ibid.,* p. 30.
23. *Ibid.,* p.76.
24. *Ibid.,* p.164.
25. *Ibid.,* p.12.
26. *Ibid.,* p.124-125.
27. V.S. Naipaul, *The Return of Eva Peron with the Killing in Trinidad.* (New York: Alfred A. Knoff, 1980, Harmondsworth; Penguin, 1981), p. 187.
28. V.S. Naipaul, *A Bend in the River, op. cit.,* p. 72.
29. *Ibid.,* p
30. *Ibid.,* p. 100-101.
31. *Ibid.,* p. 116.
32. *Ibid.,* p. 110.
33. *Ibid.,* p. 223.
34. *Ibid.,* p. 173.
35. *Ibid.,* p. 320-321.
36. Feder Lilian, *Naipaul's Truth,* (New Delhi: Indialog Publications, 2001), p. 235.

37. *A. Bend in the River, op. cit.,* p. 3.
38. See quoted in John Thieme : *The Web of Tradition,* (Reprint, Hansib Printing Ltd., 1987), p. 188.
39. *A Bend in the River, op. cit.,* p. 326.

6

Ironical Effacement of Diaspora Identity Across the Seven Seas

"We had to come out of the nightmare, and there was nowhere else to go"[1]

—V.S. Naipaul

It is a well defined truth that much of V. S. Naipaul's writings—fiction as well as non-fiction—draw on the autobiographical material and these overlapping assertions serve to present a vivid account of this author's own growth on the one hand and wounds and ailments of the expatriate Indians in their Diaspora on the other. Actually the unique combination of circumstances which related Naipaul to three societies which formed his sense and sensibility has played a prominent role in shaping the thematic matrix of his creative works. Obviously, the thematic strains that run through his oeuvre spring up from the predicament of the immigrants on the alien lands amidst the sense of chaos and turmoil. Though Naipaul discovers himself through all his works, they are also a record of the nightmarish experiences of the expatriates and their irresistible search to carve a self-esteemed niche for their identity in limbo. One can observe a marked autobiographical context to all his fiction as well as his works having his personal outlook and travel records.

In this perspective '*The Enigma of Arrival*' is Naipaul's most celebrated travel-fiction complex, perhaps what may be termed as *novelogue,* since it articulates his ordeal and evolution into a writer rather an audacious and relentlessly truthful writer travelling and observing the dynamics of the postcolonial world. This work combines the elements of fiction and non-fiction and presents a marvelous blending of autobiography with the material not directly concerned with the author's own life and personality. As Naipaul has a deep conviction in the novel form due to its seemingly indirectness to make recording this work is writer's conscious journey from the Caribbean island to the English surroundings in the countryside of Wiltshire. It interweaves the development over many years of postcolonial upheavals to shape a perspective cognizance of this diasporic writer who could peep deep into the soul and psyche of the immigrants across the seven seas. Through a fictional interaction with the history of the changing milieu, this novel picturises the metamorphosis of the author in the doubly exiled status what is the destiny of the immigrants and has no hope of any redemption from this predicament. The novel tells of an emphatic singular journey— from one place to another, from the British colony to the ancient countryside of England and from one state of mind to another—and is perhaps Naipaul's most subjective work having the complexity and richness of a novel. An analytical study of this novel classifies that Naipaul records, without rancor or nostalgia, the ravages of time on the random rural patch of Wiltshire and gradually a wholly familiar process takes on his alien perspective.

The arrival in English countryside for this young Trinidadian of Indian origin, is like a part of the postcolonial turmoil and a hope that his stranded position may derive some meaning and long cherished self-esteem here in the epicenter of the European culture. The traveler is carrying the baggage of the loss of his ancestral inheritance and the agony of his fluid life which have created a fear-psychosis in him. Moreover, the traumatic experiences in the half-made colonial societies of Trinidad have inflicted a malaise on the mind and heart of this traveler of the world. In fact, the anxiety and existential despair amidst the fluidity of life have always been agonizing him in his shameful surrounding on the island where his people have been marooned for centuries and have no hope of redemption at all. So far life could give him nothing more than deprivation and humiliation and this has resulted in despondency and morbidity. It embodies a complex of conflicting attitude towards his new environment in England based partly on a distinction between the past and the present i.e., idea and reality or emotional suffocation and intellectual inferiority. Disguised as the Narrator for the convenience of the fictional genre the author observes:

> "That idea of ruin and dereliction, of out-of-placeness, was something I felt about myself, attached to myself: a man from another hemisphere, another background, coming to rest in middle life in the cottage of a half-neglected estate, an estate full of reminders of its Edwardian past, with few connections with the present. An oddity among the estates and big houses of valley, and I, a further oddity in its grounds. I felt unanchored and strange."[2]

His solitude in the English surrounding enables him to shed the nerves of being a stranger of non-entity and strangely enough, he feels that all was well with the world and, the agony of rootlessness and nothingness is not any new curse to him; it had been heavy on his psyche even in his childhood in Trinidad. Naipaul speaks of this deep-rooted malaise as:

> "I had always lived with this idea. It was like my curse; the idea which I had even as a child in Trinidad and I had come into a world past its peak. Already I lived with the idea of death, the idea impossible for a young man to possess, to hold in his heart, that one's time on earth, one's life, was a short thing.

> These ideas of a world in decay, a world subject to constant change and of the shortness of human life, made many things bearable."[3]

This fictional travelogue expresses Naipaul's response to England and supplies images which both confirm and defy the traditional conceptions about it. It creates mysterious sensations in the writer. Jack's large house and garden and wide-spread bounty in this new background make Naipaul realize the smallness of his life in the dark alleys of Trinidad amidst the insulated and alienated people of his own community there. The smallness of his past causes him pain: the indelible impressions of the agonizing past life have made his temperament pessimistic and even amidst the richness of creativity and celebration in the English countryside the feeling of morbidity haunts him. He reiterates:

> "To see the possibility, the certainty of ruin, even at the moment of creation; it was my temperament. Those nerves had been given me as a child in Trinidad partly by our family circumstances; the half-ruined or broken-down houses, we lived in, our many moves, our general uncertainty. Possibly too, this mode of feeling went deeper, and was an ancestral inheritance, something that came with the history that had made me: not only India, with its ideas of a world outside man's control, but also the colonial plantations or estates of Trinidad, to which my impoverished Indian ancestors had been transported in the last century—estates of which this Wiltshire estate, where I now lived, had been the apotheosis."[4]

It is, however, noteworthy that Naipaul—the writer in embryo—has ambivalent feelings of loss as well as gain attributed to him by the immigration of his ancestors and then by his own move to England since his learning of English language and a specific kind of cognizance to make him a high profile writer have come from his double-exiled life in limbo. Furthermore, his passage to the imperialists' land has enkindled in him a fierce spirit to throw off his past burden so as to have a different vision and voice cut away from his linkage with his past or present loyalties. In this Eurocentric position, though aware of his ancestral Aryan culture and civilization, Naipaul finds it futile to give any historical explanation to his lost identity since all his 'Indianness' has been swallowed by the colonial absurdities in Trinidad. Gradually and firmly a feeling dawns on Naipaul that he is a *'no land's man'* without any hope of redemption from this endless exile.

In such a gruesome situation Naipaul finds it difficult to come out of this despondency. His meditation upon the English countryside, his reflections on the rural tranquility, his grave thoughts on imperial decline amongst the cottages and manor house, all tend to share the motifs of this artist who, though not native born Englishman, is gravely intended to convert and transform his inner conscience through an exercise of his creativity. A miracle happens and soon his creativity starts spreading in all directions: from his Trinidad Indian people to other Caribbean, African, South American colonies and India, the land of his origin and his journeys through these dark areas of the Third World. No doubt, the Port of Spain, the ambiance of Naipaul's childhood, could be a more concrete material to illuminate his life in England where he housed himself to inculcate his creativity at large. Now, his horizon began to be widened as the postcolonial turmoil and violence, the social duality, the strange obsessions and eccentricities of the different peoples from different races made themselves a larger world to be explored through the genre-defying works of this audacious traveler of the world. But he could also realize that to be a writer of relentless fervour and truthfulness was a Herculean task and in taking this challenge he could expect favour neither from the colonizers and nor from the colonized. Even Trinidad itself, the starting point of his life, could no longer hold him since his new journeys went on qualifying his earlier notions about this world as well as about his own selfhood.

So undoubtedly, Naipaul's *'The Enigma of Arrival'* like Eliot's *'Little Gidding'* is more than an exercise of nostalgia. How odd it would be were it be memorializing his lost life here in Wiltshire near Salisbury in the 1970s. Even if the novel contains nostalgia of the narrator for his own past then also it is so subversive that it can't be described as any emotional engagement with his ancestral culture and heritage. It is harnessed with a bleak recognition of ignorance and failure of a habitual misunderstanding of his past—an endless darkness. This hapless and hopeless situation fills Naipaul with an agony of loss and a fear of extinction and he is charged with an incessant wish to reincarnate himself into a high-spirit delineator of the truths of the present world and life especially that of the Third World expatriates. Strangely enough, there is a frankly poised contemplation of place, time, decay, change in the present life arising out of the abandoned past; of the fateful and fatal camouflaged inventions of the imperial powers. The exiled Naipaul finds himself in the miserable predicament of a doubly distanced traveler facing a crisis of losing his own individuality in this floating exile.

Being in a conflicting position, Naipaul faced the difficulty in moulding himself into an objective writer because he experienced a remarkable difference of cognizance and self-acknowledgement during these initial years in England. Soon his curiousity started spreading in different directions. Racial obsessions, socio-cultural pursuits, strange motifs and convictions of the people effected the author's sensibility and so became a larger world for Naipaul to be exposed and analysed through his literary works. Accordingly a vigorous and miraculous conviction enters into the psyche of this liberated soul to have a world of his own perspective. His solitude becomes his ordeal and gradually this ever-exiled genius inculcates a strange ability to shed his weak colonial nerves and this self-laceration leads him towards the realization of a new transformation, rather an incarnation, into a prolific writer with a miraculous vision and voice of his own kind. Amidst all the agonizing perplexities he allows himself to play lightly with the ancient Mediterranean idea that had come to him from the Chirico painting—'The Enigma of Arrival'. He, thus, decides to cleanse off all the ruins of his past from his mind and heart—if he could, and have a sort of second birth. Here comes to him at some point a sense, almost a sixth sense to articulate without any inhibition or reservation all what was uppermost in the thoughts and psyche of him and his people. Naipaul's conviction to maintain a surgeon-like objectivity could also be realized in his frank and ruthless but truthful perceptions of even his ancestral land. When he visited India he expressed the harsh realities as:

> "In travelling to India I was travelling to an un-English fantasy, and a fantasy unknown to Indians of India: I was travelling to the peasant India that my Indian grandfathers had sought to recreate in Trinidad, the 'India' I had partly grown up in, the India that was like a loose end in my mind, where our past suddenly stopped. There was no model for me here, in the exploration; neither Forster, nor Ackerley nor Kipling could help. To get anywhere in the writing, I had first of all to define myself very clearly to myself."[5]

In this way Naipaul's enigma comes to be resolved and through strange moves a *'Girmitya'* turns into a cosmopolitan who procures a penetrating vision and dauntless voice. His self-proclaimed dissociation with his past coupled with the English ambiance moulds a new found prolific writer in that man who had left the sugarcane covered island of Trinidad by renouncing even his filial ties there. He writes in this regard: "**That in the most unlikely way, at an advanced age, in a foreign country I was to find myself in tune with a landscape in a way that I had never been in Trinidad or India (both sources of different kinds of pain).**"[6] But this throwing away of his redundant past leads Naipaul into a new crisis since his temperamental despondency has entered deep into his consciousness and thought process. As a result rootlessness, violence, disintegration, alienation, and nowhereness have become more obsessing aspects of his works. This metamorphic effect of morbidity is acknowledged by him in the fifth chapter entitled 'The Ceremony of Farewell' as: **"But it was only out of this new awareness of death that I began at last to write. Death was the motif; it had perhaps been the motif along. Death and the way of handling it—that was the motif of the story of Jack."**[7]

Naipaul adopts London as the epicenter of his creative endeavours across the world. Even Trinidad, where his relations and the community people longed for meeting him, becomes almost an imaginary place at a hazy distance. Though he visits Trinidad under the compelling circumstances as on the death of his father in 1953 and that of his sister in 1984, yet he could never be allured to stay there anymore. In fact, he is deeply engrieved on the exiled and trapped destiny of his people stranded in their endless dereliction:

> "We had made ourselves a new. The world we had found ourselves in—the suburban houses with gardens, where my sister's farewell ceremony had taken place—was one had partly made ourselves and had longed for, when we had longed for money and the end of distress; we couldn't go back. There was no ship of antique shape to take us back. We had to come out of the nightmare, and there was nowhere else to go."[8]

On the sad occasion of his visit to Trinidad to mourn the death of his sister, when an old man—a distant relation of his sister's husband—boasts of the glories of their ancestral culture and religion in the Gangatic plain, Naipaul takes a pity on this egotistical sublimity which his people cherish to derive a pseudo-satisfaction from their long- dead and disintegrated past. He treats all this as an elegy on their socio-cultural death that had happened long back in 1845 when they had been indentured to Caribbean islands under the despotic rule of the British Empire. More shockingly, even the rites performed for the peace of the departed souls—all the Hindu ritualistic incantations from the Gita and other holy scriptures are only distant hollow words making no appeal to him.

However frankly enough, in spite of all his proclamation to cut off from his past and to heal the wounds caused by this ruin of his past, Naipaul could not get relief from the agonies of this irrecoverable loss. This predicament forces his forlorn spirit to realize that there is no ideal land,—no El Dorado—in the new emerging wilderness of the world and the exiled souls have to bear the ordeal amidst the existential turmoil. Therefore, in spite of his much talked Eurocentrism, Naipaul makes no final commitment to any country for his home and this stranded position and objective approach enables him to render a fairly detached account of both the colonizers as well as colonized. In this way '*The Enigma of Arrival*' dramatizes how Naipaul's pains and pleasures in his double-exiled status make him into a prolific writer and how he could convert his curse of 'nowhereness' into a boon of 'everywhereness'. The travelogue ends with the author's wonderment and staunch conviction to deal with the naked truths of this mysterious world. He contemplates as:

> "It showed me life and man as the mystery, the true religion of man, the grief and the glory. And that was, when faced with a real death, and with this new wonder about men, I laid aside my drafts and hesitations and began to write very fast about Jack and his garden."[9]

Thus, this powerful fiction- travelogue, tells in first person the story of Naipaul fleeing from the discontent and painful existence in Trinidad; of his arrival in Wiltshire and having a slow adjustment to the English milieu; of his gradual transformation and incarnation into a prolific writer liberated from all the over-possessing sentimentality or grudges. So when he talks about his ancestry there is no sentimentality; when he remembers any region of the world there is no nostalgia and in his truthful delineation he is unsparing and unyielding. This work speaks of the ordeal and evolution of Naipaul who through the process of self-laceration, sheds his jangling nerves and an audacious writer is born by experiencing the labour pains of creativity. It also records how a rare wisdom dawns on him and makes him feel that his rootlessness and homelessness are no more a curse but a blessing in disguise to rejoice himself as a citizen of the world. His trials and struggles attribute him a miraculous perspective and his new travels and speculations provide him a rare wisdom about the post colonial situation of the world. In this way *'The Enigma of Arrival'* brings a great fruit to the life of the protagonist i.e., the Narrator and the work ends on a note of celebration on resolving the enigma of identity by finding a decolonized and relentlessly truthful writer in himself.

Strangely enough, this dawning of wisdom and self-realization on this writer widens his literary horizon and enables him to look wisely on the global dimension of the problems experienced by him and his people on the alien lands. He comes to learn that the haunting fears of loss, non-entity, dereliction, fluidity of existence are not new to him since in the postcolonial era the whole world is in the grip of these maladies. On acknowledging this truth Naipaul propagates a tragic optimism to rejoice the world as it is and declares that those who fail to cope with its ways, deserve no place in it.

This autobiographical work could also be seen as an advanced re-writing of *'A House for Mr. Biswas'* since both the novels record a struggling journey towards self-hood and both do culminate in an achievement of a self-esteemed niche for their protagonists. Moreover, the first half of both ends in failure. The narrator's return to the English countryside reminds us of Mr. Biswas's return to the Tulsi house in Port of Spain in utter distress to be nursed and rejuvenated to re-start his heroic pursuit again. Mr.Biswas's tragic struggle ends in building a house for himself. Naipaul's enigma is resolved in his evolution as a giant writer. In this sense this travelogue could bring a greater fruit to the author's life and therefcre concludes on a note of celebration on finding his alternate and high profile identity.

This novel may equally be described as an attempt to deflect the painful consequences of his decision to set himself at an un-chartered distance from his own people and also of his initial inability to efface the implications of his colonial origin. It is, therefore, obvious that a ruthless exposition and dissection of the postcolonial situation in the Third World nations is more intended to heal up the wounds and ailments of the ex-colonial societies than to humiliate them. The brutal analysis of their complexities are a kind of their complacency so as to make them shoulder their responsibilities towards their nations. On individual level, Naipaul has succeeded in coming out of the enigma and indirectly he conveys his sagacious message to boost up the morale of all the immigrants—especially of the Indians—so as to make them learn this lesson to celebrating their exile.

So *'The Enigma of Arrival'* is Naipaul's powerful self-assertion which declares that its writer's rootlessness is not a burden that he carries in his Ulysses-like wanderings across the postcolonial Third World. At the same time it is his sharp weapon with which he could ironically slice up the minds and psyche of the people of these second-rated countries. Indeed this travelogue records how Naipaul could emerge as a giant writer with a broader perspective and rather an ill-reputed detachment. He is obviously a giant writer having his unique and naïve artistic skill of looking while seeing and listening while hearing all the complexities of the wilderness of the postmodern world.

Naipaul's next novel *'A Way in the World'*(1994) presents a fusion of both travel and fictional paradigms and it is a unique experience. In this novel the author, who was already engaged in creating the genre-defying literature of his own kind, has fulfilled his long cherished technique of the travel-fiction complex and it may be termed as *travelogue* or *novelogue.*

'A Way in the World' is an extremely confessional and personal account of travel experiences and autobiographical memories that spans Naipaul's entire writing career. It is made up of a series of chapters or sections uniquely connected and centering around the 'writing' process. A whole chapter is dedicated to a 'Narrator' and the writing of his 'text' whatever that might be. In fact *'A Way in the World'* reads as a complex of travel-autobiography-fiction: all of the travel strategies mentioned above have been included i.e., journalistic, ethnographic, historical, philosophical and autobiographical strategies along with Naipaul's typical fictional elements of characterization, tone and imagery. It is a narrative in the same manner as *'Finding the Centre'* dealing with the 'writer' and 'writing'. So it is a blend of different strands and Naipaul's one more experiment in his series of innovations and admixture of genres. This novel is the record of individual and writer, even if this meant trespassing the boundaries that were fixed by traditional fiction and non-fiction.

In an interview *'Delivering the Truth'* Naipaul was questioned about this book and he opined that it is a mixed kind of form; a form he chose to describe the kind of reality he wanted to in his own words:

> "This book (*A Way in the World*) is a way of dealing with all the various strands of the Caribbean or New World background, the place, and all the different stages of learning about it, as well... and the form I've arrived at seems to me truer and more natural than any artificial narrative which would have tried to create a James Michener kind of connected story. My story does have connections; they are associations. They are inseparable from the background."[10]

Naipaul has understood the meaning and significance of 'experience' for an author, the importance of 'translation' intc words of personal and external realities. Through a technique of shuttle narration, which moves the story backwards and forwards in all directions, the novelist diffuses and orients varied ideas and suggestions. When Naipaul comes face to face with an Amerindian hut and its social and natural realities, an experience occurs which is mediated through a 'cultural-ideological mind'. This represents the first 'remove' and most importantly, the actual textualisation of that 'experience' which already has a 'remove' because it has been conditioned by a culture, a society, an ideology and by memory. This is the problem of a writer; what he experiences has already been conditioned, idealogised, determined; now, further complication ensues when he is textualising that experience. Such is the case of Naipaul and his quest for the perfect 'representation or 'characterisation' of reality and involvement.

Naipaul often finds the plots for his novels in history, and the dramatic actions flow from the conflict between character and historical circumstances. This is especially true in '*A Way in the World*' in which history is intricately woven with fiction. Naipaul has artistically meshed together literature and history e.g., dialogue, characterization, technique of narrative and the historical perspectives of time and space. As Subramani has observed: **"Naipaul has combined the apparently dichotomous task of the historian who depicts individuals to illuminate historical process or historical period, and the novelist who is interested in individual psychology and morality."**[11] Historical allusions, facts and autobiography are fastidiously intertwined in fictional passages also. The typical Naipaulian imageries abound as:

> "The fires of the rubbish dump burned night and day. The smoke was black turning to dark brown; it often billowed over the highway; the smell was high; you had to turn up your car windows. The people of the shanty town, men and women and children worked in this smoke—emblematic silhouettes—raking over the rubbish for things that could be salvaged and sold. The local corbeaux, black, heavy, hunched hopped about the slopes of rubbish; the children of the shanty town ran between the traffic on the rubbish- strewn highway to get to the dump."[12]

The ethnographic detail is also fastidiously wrought out as the following passages do reveal and illustrate:

> "Once or twice during the day we stopped at an Amerindian village. At these village sites the river bank was higher, with a ramp or path zigzagging down to where the village dugouts were tied up. The people were pale, black hair. Animated among themselves, exchanging food and goods and news, they managed at the next moment to be distant with the rest of us: holding themselves with an extraordinary stillness on their tree-shaded bank, and looking down without expression at the boat."[13]

> "Some of the women are making cassava bread. Finished rounds are on the grass roof. At the side of the kitchen hut hangs the long plaited tube which can be twisted or wrung by means of a horizontally fitted stick, to squeeze the poison out of grated cassava: a poison caught in a wooden dish on the ground. Because this poison is valuable: it can preserve meat upto a year." [14]

There is a section of the novel which gives an account of Columbus's discovery of the islands, he gives information about the origin of the name Trinidad. It is, in fact, a series of linked narratives, moving backward and forward as per the requirement of the story and the convenience of the novelist. In terms of narrative technique and style, *'A Way in the World'* is and will probably be considered Naipaul's lasting masterpiece, going beyond his early fictional narratives and the lively and warm narration keeps the novel alive. Sarafin Roldon Santiago writes in this regards as:

> *"A Way in the World"* represents a text that has totally integrated the three categories discussed in this paper: the travelogue technique, the autobiographical sense, and the fictional elements. These three areas had always seemed to be working together in Naipaul's

narratives, but in his later writings, they have been vulcanized and totally integrated."[15]

In fact a brief biography of the author can be constructed out of the statements of his books and *'A Way in the World'* is no exception. It has been his quest of a life-time journey, a travel into self, time and space in which Naipaul, the author, the protagonist, the narrative voice and the principal character have blended together, have coalesced. Against the backdrop of colonial history, Naipaul also throws light on the situation in the postcolonial world. And for Naipaul, the author and humanist, the whole wide world is a fictional arena replete and bubbling over with characters and stories ready to be experienced, ready to be textualised from the people he found himself among.

With *'A Way in the World'* Naipaul's literary career had come to a temporary halt, but his next appealing novel *'Half a Life'* published in October 2001, again reiterates and depicts the agony and dilemma of the immigrants in the wilderness of the alien land—the favourite theme with Naipaul. Interweaving the tales of three generations of an Indian Brahmin family *'Half a Life'* is the story of a race in search of a familiar face in the mirror of time. The irony, however, lies in the fact that the mirror reflects the images which are weird and not even recognizable.

As Naipaul is a world champion writer of the theme of dislocation, disintegration and consequent loss of identity—the recurring theme in the literature of Diaspora—through the story of Willie Somerset Chandran, *'Half a Life'* also reiterates this ironical existence and despair of the desperate Indians across the seven seas. Just as in *'The Mystic Masseur'* Ganesh Ramasumair's search for roots takes him to various stages of transformation and finally the face that he could discover is that of G. Ramsay Muir, and Mohan Biswas's search for a house is a metaphor for his search for selfhood in the mirror of time,*'Half a Life'* is apparently an extension of this incessant quest recorded through the search of Willie Somerset Chandran for his face and identity in limbo. This novel presents two sets of father son stories each of whom has his own fears, his own solitariness and his own loss but sadly there is no channel of communication between them and their disintegration is inevitable destiny. Out of these three, however, it is only the youngest one – the protagonist who is given a name even. His father and grandfather, despite having strongly influenced his story, are left anonymous – again a symbolic presentation of loss of identity.

The novel opens with the beginning of Willie Somerset Chandran's search for his roots as he awakes one day to the realization that his middle name sounds alien. He asks his father; **'Why is my middle name Somerset?'**[16] This question regarding the very essence of a person's existence brings into light the irony of Willie's background of his half-life in half-made societies with the people who are themselves leading a life which is half-realised, half-discovered and half-lived. Willie's quarry unleashes a torrent of memories unfolding before him a complicated picture which relates to his roots. A probing look reveals that this man is as much an amalgam of drastically different traits as is his name an admixture of different and even antagonistic streams. It is his destiny that half of his name does not belong to him; it is borrowed from the famous writer Somerset Maugham; his first name proclaims him as a Christian whereas his surname signifies his mixed ancestry. It is this revelation that breeds contempt in the mind of this twenty year old son of a half-rebel Brahmin father and a low caste mother. His incompleteness becomes the cause of his self-hatred and thus begins Willie's attempt to run away from the shadow of his past. His low parental status instills in him a sense of shame and he resolves to survive by shedding off the ignoble past as he attempts to live in a world of falsehood and make-believe identity. But past is a shadow one can never betray and in the vain attempt to wash one's hands of the past, one always stakes one's present and future. Willie's search for his roots takes him backward because his roots are entwined with those of his father and grandfather. His story is set up in post-independent

India, then in London and then he travels to a pre-independence African country which is closely modeled on Mozambique and then for a brief period appears in Berlin. The first thirty-five pages of the novel constitute Willie's father's story, then almost hundred pages are a record of Willie's struggle for existence in London and remaining part of the novel, apart from a brief tarriance in Berlin, records his life in Africa which in Naipaul's words is only a land of bush. Willie feels at home with many people he comes close during his travels because they are also leading a half-life in exile and are faceless like him. But these are all his chance acquaintances and in his vain attempt to find his face in limbo, he ironically loses even the half-life that was within his reach.In this regard Asha Chubey has explained the cause of the incompleteness of this protagonist as: **"The cultural as well as social alienation that Willie Chandran undergoes in England and then in Mozambique takes its roots in cultural alienation which is more pronounced as parental alienation."**[17]

Willie's socio-cultural disintegration begins in his childhood and leads to his persistent attempts to negate his weird self and to find some other concrete image even if it is made of falsehood. His whole life is doomed by the scar of his father's misplaced ideal in marrying a low caste woman and initiating the alienation which brings punishment to descending generation. Cultural alienation is in Willie's blood because his father had revolted against the tradition and negated the history by marrying a low caste woman. Those were the times of the national movement and the impact of Gandhi was in air. Gandhi's call was for the upliftment of the neglected segment of society—the untouchables who were discriminated against, and Willie's father—the son of priest decided to marry a low caste woman simply to show acquiescence to the ideal of sacrifice. There was no question of love; instead the very sight of the girl bred repulsion. The austerity and discipline imposed on senior Chandran by his father had bred immense dissatisfaction in him and his restless soul was yearning for an anchor. Years later, he tells his son Willie: "**I was in a great mess feeling that we were all living in a false security, feeling idle, hating my studies and knowing that great things were happening outside.**"[18] The passivity of his ancestry appeared death-like while the prospects of getting in an arranged marriage and taking up a secure job seemed uninspiring and unchallenging. It was a maddening impulse which sought satisfaction only in destroying itself. Negating history is a sin and Willie's father had to bear the punishment for his foolish decision to become a scapegoat for his people with vested interests and illusionary ideals. In Willie's father's case tradition takes its revenge by pulling him back to its clutches. Despite all his contempt for his father, Willie's father takes sanctuary in a temple and becomes a mendicant. This disgusting story, told by his father in reply to Willie's question, creates contempt in the heart of son who is destined to bear the burden of this cursed ancestry on him. Being a half-Brahmin he can not relate fully to the low caste and being a low caste mother's son he is not complete and whole heartedly acceptable in Brahmin community.

This half-ness of Willie's identity leads him to reject his roots and to make desperate attempts to create a new image of selfhood for which he travels all around. Willie hopes to reverse the tradition when he decides to go outside the periphery of his ancestral establishment for searching a meaningful identity away from conservative mould of his parental existence. This break from the past pushes Willie into a limbo in which position he keeps dangling for many years to come. It is ironical and enigmatic that in trying to find a new identity Willie sets another much more complicated and faceless mould for himself wherefrom escape is not possible. Willie's defiant soul takes a destructive and negative approach as he decides to dissolve his past without knowing its repercussions.

With the very inception of the novel, Naipaul sympathetically projects the mental make-up of Willie and his sister; they seem to be fairly confused and mutilated and remain tongue-tied as the class teacher asks what does his father do? This unforgettable event at the school keeps on rankling at the back of the protagonist's mind for a fairly long time. Obviously for Willie Chandran growing up is a process motivated by self-hatred and despise and when he has to write an English composition in school, he gives vent to all his pent up contempt against his father and his family background by presenting himself as a Canadian with a western way of life. He writes an invented story which is based on the bits of life he has known through an American story book. Father in that composition becomes Pop and mother becomes Mom. In attempting to free himself from his half-ness Willie creates a world of falsehood. Asha Choubey writes:

> "Willie's pretentions of having been born of a Canadian father tantamounts to getting rid of his Indian father whom he is ashamed of. Although he replaces his low caste mother with a Canadian Mom but here the intent seems to get rid of the real mother as to present the fictitious Canadian father in an authentic setting with a suitable counterpart."[19]

Willie's hatred for his parents goes deep in his psyche and it is apparent in his reluctance to show this composition to his father. The realization comes to the father thus: **"But I have him nothing. He is not me. He is his mother's son."**[20] A week is passed in tension with Willie and father both eyeing each other in suspicion. The son wants his father to realize his blunder and when this solace is not granted he despises his father much more than ever. This hatred and tension eliminates in Willie's second composition 'King Cophetua and the Beggar Maid' in which he strikes harder on this monstrous parenthood. In this story he projects his mother as a beggar woman who becomes the queen of Cophetua when the king marries her for her surpassing beauty. Soon begins her humiliation at the hands of her husband, his family and even that of the courtiers. In the mean time the couple is blessed with a son who grows up with the sufferings faced by his mother and deeply felt by him. On growing up this son kills Cophetua. The message of the story is quite loud and clear and his father does not fail to see it. He thinks: "**We've created a monster.....The boy will poison what remains of my life. I must get him far away from here.**"[21] The fire of the hatred burns in full when Willie fuels it by writing his third and last composition. The deficient father now realizes that their life is merely an existence in alienation and this miserable predicament is distorting the emotions of his son and to avert further harm to himself he thinks it a need of the hour to allow the estranged son to go in his own direction. He expresses his observation in this regard as:

> "I used to think that you were me and I was worried at what I had done to you. But now I know that you are not me. What is in my head is not in yours. You are somebody else, somebody I don't know and I worry for you because you are launched on a journey I know nothing of."[22]

Willie's hatred induces him to negate his roots and this sense of alienation makes him a 'sojourner'. He goes to London to find out some new identity and socio-cultural face which may free him of all the humiliating bondages with his ignoble past. But it is ironical that his search for some comfortable and complete identity proves futile and he loses even his half-life since there he finds himself in the predicament of nowhereness and meaninglessness. In London Willie is lost and the education he gets there is absolutely devoid of authenticity and perspective for life. He pursues everything half-heartedly in a state of fluidity in limbo. The novelist explains his situation as:

> "The learning he was being given was like the food he was eating, without savour. The two were inseparable in his mind "And just as he ate without pleasure, so, with a kind of blindness, he did what

> the lectures and tutors asked of him, read the books and articles and did the essays. He was unanchored, with no idea of what lay ahead."[23]

In the fluidity of existence in London, Willie is drawn to the 'bohemian' immigrant community of the post-war city, its dingy West-End clubs, lonely pavements and odd sexual escapades. Floating in the bottomless sea of multiculturalism, Willie comes to realize the gruesome consequences of his distance and freedom from his tradition. For the purpose of gaining a new image he has lost his old face and now floats in uncertainty with no hope of revival. It is not only Willie, almost all the expatriates are in the miserable predicament of no entity, uncertainty and alienation. In London Willie seems to have found his ground for a while when, all of a sudden, he comes to a reconciliation and realization that he did not need to rebel for the simple reason that distance from his root socio-cultural background has left him unanchored and in a state of unbridles freedom. In search of his identity in this strange world Willie adopts the defence mechanism of projecting a borrowed, make-believe identity and ventures to live with this superficial image once again:

> "...he adapted certain things he had read, and he spoke of his mother as belonging to an ancient Christian community of the subcontinent, a community almost as old as Christianity itself. He kept his father as a Brahmin. He made his father's father a 'courtier'. So playing with words, he began to re-make himself. It excited him and began to give him a feeling of power."[24]

While making his efforts to settle in London, Willie realizes that there are numerous immigrants there leading a bohemian life in the limbo in their own eccentric ways. There is Percy Cato, a Jamaican of mixed parentage and more brown than black. Percy is, in many ways Willie, ashamed of his background and instead of presenting facts about his life he also believes in creating fictitious stories to have a face image to project amongst the people who are also heterogeneous and rootless like him. He tells Willie that his father went to Panama as a clerk to which Willie reacts with a self-experienced complexity of falsehood: "**That is foolish story. His father went there as a laborer. He would have been in one of the gangs, holding his pickaxe before him on the ground, like the others, and looking obediently at thephotographer.**"[25] This fictional recreation of their backgrounds as well as their overwhelming sense of dressing up provides these exiled derelicts a kind of false shelter from their rootless realities which they want to wash away from their minds.

Moreover, when Willie takes these immigrants close to his heart and hopes for some emotional support, they shrink away giving only a few words of formality. This plight of helplessness and lack of belongingness causes more pain and fear-psychosis to Willie than his real half-life identity. Quite expectedly, the physical distance from his parents revives the affinity to his father and first signs of this realization are visible in his composition at London College in which he keeps his parental ground quite close to reality. Willie, who had not forgiven his father even in stories, now realizes that life after all was not easy for his father also. On being disillusioned with a bohemian life in limbo Willie earns a wisdom as he speaks: "**I misjudged my father. I used to think that the world was easy for him as a Brahmin and that he became a fraud out of idleness. Now I began to understand how hard the world must have been for him.**"[26]

This rediscovered shadow of his father figure, now keeps haunting Willie in all the weak as well as the strong moments of his life hereafter. He is split within himself and is in a dilemma of internal conflict in his bid to achieve assimilation or acculturation which is the only option left to the alienated immigrant in the alien society where he or she is merely a marginalized vagrant. Sexual promiscuity is witnessed in the Third World immigrants living in the liberal Western World as an existential activity with no sense of permanence and the inhibitions and taboos of the parochial society have no reason to survive at all.

But whatever freedom Willie attempts to enjoy in the Notting Hill culture, is unsatisfactory because his cultural background and awareness of incompleteness has bred inhibitions in him. He is a man doomed to live under a shadow of his hazy past which has disappeared for ever. Even the sexual frustrations experienced by him are not new to him; they are the frustrations of a marooned race of a disintegrated society and of a lost culture. Therefore, Willie is divided and disintegrated under the pressures of cultural schizophrenia; in this sense a state of divided identity—divided by history, culture and existential pursuits in the circumstances.

So Willie's attempts to enjoy in the Notting Hill culture, brings only frustration and anxiety because every authentic satisfaction comes from the mental state which is distorted in the wilderness of the rootless life. Even the girls with whom Willie sleeps are not his friends but the so-called lovers of his so-called friend and his sexual involvements also lead him nowhere except the despondency. Willie goes on planning to declare his love whereas Jane marries her childhood friend and leaves him in the lurch. Perdita, who happens to be Richard's girl friend leaves Willie's side after finding no satisfaction in the one night sexual encounter with him. His repeated sexual failures make him realize that his mind can't get pleasure until and unless he re-establishes his affinity with his father whom he misses every minute now. He realizes: **"When my father told me his life story and talked about his sexual impotence I mocked him. I was a child then. Now I discover I am like my poor father."**[27]

Another important factor in the diasporic existence is that the language is the power of expression and life is meaningless unless it is experienced and comprehended appropriately. Naipaul seems to convey that displacement brings the dispossession of the language power and thus aggravates the sense of alienation. The immigrant is always at a disadvantage in the foreign land and his escape depends on the degree of his adaptability to those aspects which are essentially alien to him. None but Naipaul could understand the agony of losing one's culture and language and in case of Willie the loss of proper language is ironically painful since he is emerging as a writer. On the publication of his first book Willie is introduced as **"a subversive new voice from the subcontinent."**[28] With his remigration to African country Willie's voice itself becomes a victim to the despotic forces. While traveling to Ana's African country from Southampton Willie's mind is occupied by the confusions that are caused by such frequent changes in the setting. The novelist writes: **"Willie was trying to deal with the knowledge that had come to him on the ship that his home language had almost gone, that his English was going, that he had no proper language, no gift of expression."**[29] Actually Willie had come to find some substantial identity and future in the western world of creative writing but on failing to find one he traverses to Africa which seems to bear more affinity than the West. In drifting away from one place to another, from one continent to another and from one ambiance to another Willie comes to realize that he is incurring the loss of his identity as well as language. Thus the quest for identity pushes the 'subaltern' towards silence and oblivion.

Even his relationship with Ana is based on the similarity of their predicament in alien surroundings. While hunting desperately for wholeness and authenticity in life, Willie discovers a kind of reciprocity in Ana and the half-ness in both the expatriates strikes a bond and mutual attraction with a hope of finding completeness through entering into a merger on physical level. Strangely enough, the half-ness of Ana makes him forget his own lacking and, though temporarily, her company strengthens and allows him to push back the shadow of inadequacy which otherwise looms large in his life. The third person narrator remarks thus: **"What was most intoxicating for Willie was that for the first time in his life he felt himself in the presence of someone who accepted him completely. It spoilt**

everything."[30] Willie goes with Ana to the African country with all expectations to belong there but it is ironical that his fate becomes more than worst in his floatsam existence. Though the description of the land is modeled on Mozambique, Naipaul maintains the anonymity to intensify the sense of limbo in the existential predicament of the protagonist. Walking in the streets of the town he feels that he is '**walking as if in wilderness.**'[31] Willie becomes a 'nowhere man' and he reflects on his loss of belongingness: **"I don't know where I am. I don't think I can pick up my way back. I don't ever want this view to become familiar. I must not unpack. I must never behave as though I am staying.**"[32] In spite of the agony of being a non-entity and loss of belongingness even here, Willie has no destination to go with any hope of betterment and despite initial reluctance he stays for eighteen years. Describing his fate to Sarojini, his sister in India, he explains that in Africa, in hope of finding a niche for himself, he did experience the loss of whatever little selfhood he had in London. In London, at least, he was known as Willie Chandran but in Africa he is reduced simply to **"Ana's London man.**"[33]

In his efforts to wipe away the stigma of his historical past inferiority, Willie goes in the wilderness of double exile and procures nothing except a more painful status of being in the fluidity of existence and lack of recognition as an individual. He has faced an agonizing trauma of deracination and marginalization just like so many other uprooted people of mixed race and un-pedigreed class. Despite all the unpleasant and weird experiences that have reached deep in his psyche, Willie gradually finds that this is the absurd situation of the existence of so many derelicts who are infested with the same disease of the colossal loss in exile of the Third World nations and even in the double exile in England. So he, gradually, finds solace in realizing that he is not the only one bearing the burden of nothingness and nowhereness. He discovers that he has **"a half-and-half world and half- and-half friends.**"[34] However, in spite of all sense of loss and all pains of alienation, Willie feels much at home among the

Africans. In his words:"**In Africa I had after a while let those London lies drop, in our half-and-half group for a while, seemed to have no points.**"[35] Willie, at least for a while, seems to have come to terms with himself in his weird and indefinable identity.

The dilemma that the lack of belongingness infuses, is the destiny of those colonizers also ,who have willingly or unwillingly decided to be left behind in the ex-colonies. Graca, the beautiful wife of Luis stayed back in Africa when the Portuguese left the country. Graca is a third generation descendent of these colonizing people since her grandfather had come to Africa with the colonizing mission of his country but stayed back. Even she faces a crisis of identity as she lives in Africa and her children, on returning to Portugal, have to provide documentary proof to ascertain their identity. Actually loss of identity is an inevitable evil in an exiled life irrespective of the background of the immigrants. Willie comes to understand this plain truth in course of time and at forty one, after having spent eighteen years in Africa, he realizes that he has allowed himself to become an easy victim to the slippery substances. On a rainy day when he slips it comes to him as a realization that it is high time to stop making a fool of himself. Resolving to come out of the shadow of the image of 'Ana's London Man' he tells Ana as:"**I mean I've given you eighteen years. I can't give you any more. I can't live your life any more. I want to live my own.**"[36] He further realizes that Ana is also a sufferer of the same disease since she has herself been leading a borrowed life. She tells Willie of almost the similar situation: **"Perhaps, it wasn't really my life either.**"[37]

Quest for identity has a broad spectrum meaning and it has been manifested in various ways in the will to exist despite all odds and to survive all odds. Dwelling upon the recurring theme of dislocation and consequent loss of identity in this novel Asha Choubey writes:

> "*Half a Life* is the story of a race in search of a familiar face in the the mirror; the irony however

> lies in the fact that even the mirror reflects a face which is not recognizable. Through the story of William Somerset Chandran Naipaul presents the ironical existence of diaspora.[38]

The stigma of being a second rated citizen hangs around Willie like the albatross around the ancient mariner's neck in *'The Ancient Mariner'*. In Africa he is not only one bearing the burden of the albatross, there are many like him who are infested with a sense of double exile. He discovers that he is in a half-and-half world with half-and-half friends who had come to reconcile with their position as people of the second rank.

Thus *'Half a Life'* shows a surpassing emotional conflict, an agony of separation and pathos of yearning for what is lost; a futile search for El Dorado which leads nowhere. Whereas *'The Enigma of Arrival'* picturises Naipaul's own conflict, crisis and his ultimate growth as a writer, *'Half a Life'* must be judged as 'coming of age and wisdom to Naipaul's progressive hero figure who is desperate to carve a new respectable image in the mirror of time in limbo. This self-realisation of the protagonists in his successive novels leads us to conclude that Naipaul's fiction may be having a continuity in their progressive dramatization of the immigrants' quest for selfhood in alien existence.

This thread of inter-woven progress and continuity of thematic perspective could actually be seen in his other works also since they derive their strength and inspiration from Naipaul's lived experiences. It will, therefore, not be any exaggeration to say that the protagonists of his novels may differ in many ways but basically and essentially they all are the faces of one symbolic figure—an exiled Indian immigrant in limbo restlessly searching for some alternate self-image in the mirror of time. The crises and predicaments of the heroes of his fictional world picturise the different stages of this epical search of the expatriates in the alien surroundings. Naipaul's confessional statement in an interview with Ronald Bryden in 1973 justifies this notion as he has proclaimed: **"All my work is really one work. I'm really writing one big book."**[39]

All the major protagonists of Naipaul's novels suffer the tragedy of displacement, disintegration and separation from their land and Naipaul seems to share vicariously this predicament of his struggling heroes. Willie in Naipaul's twelfth novel may be in many ways different from Ganesh Ramsumair in *'The Mystic Masseur'*,Mohan Biswas in *'A House for Mr. Biswas'* and Ralph Singh in *'The Mimic Men'* but essentially they all are one as they present different aspects of the immigrant Indians' socio-cultural mindset and psychological implications. To say, the separation from their land leads to inner conflict and split as the forlorn spirits wander in the wilderness of the rootless world and their epical search for order and authenticity in life leads them nowhere to exist in limbo. The first hand experience of this novelist expresses his own enigma and heroic exploit to carve an authentic identity and to shape a relentlessly truthful writer in the same ambiance.

References

1. V.S. Naipaul. *The Enigma of Arrival. op. cit.,* p. 385.
2. *Ibid.,* p. 13.
3. *Ibid.,* p. 23.
4. *Ibid.,* p. 55.
5. *Ibid.,* p. 167-168.
6. *Ibid.,* p. 189.
7. *Ibid.,* p. 376.
8. *Ibid.,* p. 385.
9. *Ibid.,* p. 387.
10. 'Delivering the Truth', Interview by Aamer Hussein, *Times Literary Supplement,*(Sept. 2, 1994), p. 3-4.
11. Subramani, 'Historical Consciousness in V.S. Naipaul,' *New Literary Review,*15(1988), p. 31.
12. V. S. Naipaul, *A Way in The World,* (New York: Vintage, 1995), p. 37.

13. *Ibid.*, p. 46.
14. *Ibid.*, p. 64.
15. Serafin Roldan Santiago, 'V.S. Naipaul's Vulcanisation Travel and Fiction Paradigms', *V.S. Naipaul: Critical Essays,* Vol. 1, (ed), Mohit K.Ray, (Nrw Delhi: Atlantic Publishers & Distributors, 2002), p. 200.
16. V.S.Naipaul, *Half a Life* (London: Picador 2001), p. 1.
17. Asha Chubey, 'Naipaul's Half a Life: Coming to Terms with King Cophetua', *V.S. Naipaul: Critical Essays,* Vol. 2, ed. Mohit K.Ray. *op. cit.,* p.168.
18. V.S. Naipaul, *Half a Life, op. cit.,* p.19.
19. Asha Choubey, op. cit., p. 172.
20. V.S.. Naipaul ,*Half a Life, op. cit.,* p.41.
21. *Ibid.*, p.43.
22. *Ibid.*, p.49.
23. *Ibid.*, p.23.
24. *Ibid.*, p.61.
25. *Ibid.*, p.62.
26. *Ibid.*, p.58.
27. *Ibid.*, p.118.
28. *Ibid.*, p.122.
29. *Ibid.*, p.132.
30. *Ibid.*, p. 125.
31. *Ibid.*, p.134.
32. *Ibid.*, p.135.
33. *Ibid.*, p.145.
34. *Ibid.*, p.162.
35. *Ibid.*, p.179.
36. *Ibid.*, p.136.
37. *Ibid.*, p.138
38. Asha Choubey, 'A Critique of Naipaul's *Half a Life* : Searching for Identity in Limbo',*V.S. Naipaul: Critical Essays,* Vol. 1 ,Ed. Mohit K. Ray, *op. cit.,* p. 227.
39. Interview by Ronald Bryden, 'The Novelist V.S. Naipaul About His Works', *Listener,* 89 (March 22, 1973), p. 367.

7

Summing-up

"The world is what it is; men who are nothing, who allow themselves to become nothing, have no place in it."[1]

V.S. Naipaul

The foregoing chapters analyze the making up of V.S. Naipaul's mindset as a prolific writer with a peculiar literary sensibility and also present a critical study of the thematic aspects of his novels which articulate the tragic disintegration and loss of the immigrants and their persistent quest for identity and authenticity in the alien surroundings. The aim of this analytical study and inquiry about the vision and sensibility of this high profile Nobel Laureate as well as about the theme of his genre-defying books has been to focus on the predicament of the immigrants, especially the Indians indentured during the colonial reign of the British Crown. Actually an articulation of the human consequences of colonialism, of the wounds inflicted on the heart and psyche of the colonized peoples and of the predicament of all the immigrants in general and the Asians in particular, has been the major concern of Naipaul both in his fictional as well as non-fictional works.

No doubt, the darkest crimes against humanity were

perpetrated during the colonial rule in the Third World nations and the distress, agony and anguish of the colonized people resulted in disintegration and complications both at the individual as well as the social levels. The colonial myth of '*The Whiteman's Burden*' and the education provided by the colonizing masters in the colonies conditioned the mind and psyche of the colonized peoples, especially of those indentured away in never-ending exile, in such a way that they came to believe in the superiority of their patron colonizers and accepted their own status as inferior beings of the deficient folk. The miserable predicament of the expatriates has been picturised by recreating the milieu of the West Indies where so many indentured Indians are lost in the wilderness of the modern times. Due to the massive transportation of the Indians to the West Indies colonies, there they were thrown into void to face the problems of rootlessness, displacement, homelessness and a consequent disintegration and all this forced these expatriates to desperately grapple for a foothold in alien environment. The socio-cultural disintegration and alienation reduced these immigrants to the status of 'derelict' people robbed of their originality and hence instilled with inferiority and dependency syndromes. Moreover, the long exposure to the Creole culture and the complex amalgam of various peoples deracinated these immigrants and their mimicry tendencies are the inevitable consequences of the colonization. V. S. Naipaul has portrayed this phenomenon of the socio-cultural disintegration which maimed the soul and psyche of these immigrants in a severe way. Being a Trinidad born Indian, Naipaul speaks largely from his lived experiences and weird memories in the colonial as well as postcolonial situations. He has rendered a more accurate and truthful picture of the uprooted and rootless Asians, more specifically Indians, in their exiled destiny surrounded by the peoples coming from different races and colours . Naipaul has proved himself a relentless delineator committed to truth and objectivity and has presented a vivid description of the crises of the colonized people with a precision because it came from his own tragic and gruesome experiences as a displaced person in an endless exile.

The introductory chapter of this book focuses on the enigmatic and complex identity and fate of V.S. Naipaul as an individual and as a writer because, in spite of being associated with no less than three socio-cultural backgrounds – Indian by ancestry, Trinidadian by birth and English by adaptation—he has been unable to find his moorings in any of them. Though renouncing his filial ties with his ever exiled '*Girmitiya*' community in Trinidad and living mainly in his private hermitage in English countryside, this prolific dissenter makes no final commitment to any land for his identity and this audacity has enabled him to render a fairly detached account his existence in Diaspora by proclaiming himself a citizen of the world. The second chapter investigates Naipaul's much talked Euro-centrism, his sagacious insight into the tragic distortions of the past of his community and his self-procured wisdom to transform himself into a relentlessly truthful and high profile delineator of the postcolonial situation of the modern world. As Naipaul is an extraordinary writer having a multifaceted personality enriched by his lived experiences in multiple socio-cultural backgrounds, his creative works are also constantly progressive in theme and genre-defying in technique and style. Having a terrifying passion for truth, even if it is sour, Naipaul argues his ways through the treacherous alleys of the half-made colonial societies of the Third World and his forceful imagination is inseparable from the wreckage of history and the existential struggle of the Diaspora. With a literary career of spanning half a century and more than 30 genre-defying books, Naipaul's entire contribution to literature is spiraling round and round the expatriate themes which are central to his creative effusions. No doubt, he is a writer with much talked 'Eurocentric' sensibility but it is equally true that he is defiant and audaciously objective in his observations and assertions and also does not spare form slicing either the colonized or the colonizers in his dissection. None can deny the truth that V.S. Naipaul, with London as the base of his creativity, has contributed voluminously and qualitatively to the main stream of the postcolonial literature. However, London remained the land of his literary exercises and the main stuff of his works has been procured from his lived experiences and from his journeys across the Third World nations, especially Trinidad—his birth place, and India—the original land of his ancestors. Indeed, Naipaul's literature originated from his own odd situation as a twice exiled writer who is never restricted by the national boundaries; his freedom is accentuated by his existential status of an audacious giant who doesn't miss home. This writer constantly challenges the received wisdom of time in dealing with the predicament of the uprooted immigrants and at the same time maintains a surgeon-like objectivity while dissecting the complex perspectives of the societies and the cultures in his creative endeavours. Therefore, when he remembers any region of the world, there is no nostalgia, when he talks about his ancestry, there is no sentimentality and when he slices up any socio-cultural group of people, he never bothers about his appraisal or criticism at all. He is innovative, mysteriously interesting and relentlessly truthful in delineating the hopes and aspirations, fears and frustrations and anxieties and challenges experienced by the expatriates in the alien surroundings. However, the limitations of Naipaul have also been clearly exposed and strictly defined since sometimes he speaks like a perverted scholar and defiles the grace and glory of Indian saints, sculptures and giants having high cultural values. For instance, the criticism and mockery of Mahatma Gandhi,Vinoba, Nirad C. Choudhary and Nehru is an unpardonable offence committed by this Narcissistic and egotistical writer of the postmodern time. This severe attitude towards India and more than often mockery of every person or thing of India seems to be the distortions caused by his English sense and sensibility and he occasionally proves himself merely a pampered child of the West. That is why in present time this, otherwise literary giant, has become more intolerable and too offensive to be accepted. William Dalrylimple is quite right in rejecting the ego-indulgence of Naipaul as he declares the nature of this writer sick with contempt and so declares it the need of the hour to eliminate this writer. Similarly, S. Prassanarajan stressed on this obsession of Naipaul and declared that Naipaul is the chronicler of colonial imperfections and he entered into a Faustian deal with the colonizers. So, I find nothing wrong in assessing Naipaul an affected and Narcissistic person possessing the prides and prejudices of a spoiled intellectual of the present world. This notion about this pervert literary giant possessing a rare magical language and highly convincing arguments, got further strength when only two years back his confessional biography *'The World is What It is'* revealed a lot of the indelible scars and blots on his character. No doubt, if such a controversial writer criticises our legendry saint Gandhi or other sculptors of modern India he deserves condemnation, if not the assassination as professed by Dalrymple. Here, my humble submission is that there is a tragic flaw in this literary giant as he does not hesitate in sacrificing even to Gandhi and to our world renowned cultural and spiritual heritage perhaps only to scale greater heights as a writer of denunciations.

So far as the question of Naipaul's nationality is concerned, he does not make any final commitment to any land and has perhaps stations himself at a position from where he could have quite a good view of all the sides of the world. To say the truth, he maintains his narcissistic entity stranded above all the earthly overshadowing prides and prejudices and so rejoices the freedom of a decolonized citizen of the world. However, his intellectual bent is towards the western habits of thought and he seems to be overpowered by the metropolitan values and so somehow smells 'Anglophile'. But a probing study of Naipaul's creative works and interviews clarify that, being thrown out in limbo by destiny, this restless spirit went on a long voyage in time and space and that too—a pointless and endless one. His enigmatic existence along with the whole of his West Indies experiences enkindled in him a wish to be a completely decolonized and globally acknowledged literary giant who, through his creative oeuvre, could attempts to understand his past so as to come to terms with it, and to some extent, to silence and mitigate his nagging awareness of not being too close to India but also not too far from her. The early separation from the parents bred in him a deep sense of rootlessness, alienation, desolation and loss of identity that eventually sprouted into a rare sensibility for extensive readings and travellings with a self-proclaimed freedom of vision and voice. Strange metamorphosis happened to Naipaul and the stress of non-entity and insecurity in the exiled life procured a wild passion for creativity. Resultantly, the personal cognizance of Naipaul became a collective consciousness of the expatriates and got the emotional as well as the rational manifestation in his works at large.

Therefore, Naipaul has a complete innovative voice and vision representing the beginning of the great shift in ethnicity in English letters that could eventually see the triumph of Diaspora writers such as Salman Rushdie, Ben Okrai, Zadie Smith, Kiran Desai and so on. To say the truth, Naipaul is a relentless delineator and even dissenter who exposes the inner truths of both the colonizers and the colonized with same dexterity and to assign him any nationality is insufficient as well as unacceptable to him. The literary establishments took a while to catch up with the sharp edge of Naipaul's writings but, by now, he has become a too towering literary figure to be confined to any patch of land or any strict nationality at all. So, today he is a writer of world-wide repute and has got the stature of a completely decolonized and international citizen of the world and the Naipaul cult has many fanatic followers and awestruck emulators all over the world.

The first four novels, explored in the third chapter of this book, draw mainly on Naipaul's boyhood in Trinidad and hence present a poignant picture of the immigrant Indians' struggle to preserve their historical identity and also their unconscious disintegration there. These novels deal with the gradual collapse of the insulated Indian culture and the complexity of mimicry and the crisis of identity confronted by these uprooted people. It is also said that by dealing with the colossal loss of 'Indianness' in Trinidadian background Naipaul has written off his debts to his ancestral past before severing his umbilical cord with India. However, it will be more appropriate to assess these early novels as a manifestation of psychological self-laceration in an alien environment and through an imaginative re-creation of the past the author has attempted to reconcile with the predicament of the present. These novels, especially '*A House for Mr. Biswas*', are dominated by autobiographical elements and the recordings of the East Indians' displacement, alienation and flotsam existence are simultaneously author's quest for identity as well as his potent weapon to expose the cultural colonization of the half-made societies in the Third World. There is also a thematic linkage in these novels that serves to recreate the socio-cultural background of Trinidad. '*The Mystic Masseur*' focuses on the rural background, '*The Suffrage of Alvira*' deals with its multiracial aspect and '*Miguel Street*' completes the picture by focusing on the urban picaroon world of Port of Spain. The meteoric rise and metamorphosis of the protagonists in these novels symbolize the peculiar traits emerging in the Indian community undergoing this process of disintegration in exile.

A close perusal of these novels makes clear the crucial role played by the western education and also by the American presence on the West Indies islands during the Second World War. The duality created by the western education in the lives of the colonized people of the East Indian community is evident in the character of Ganesh who follows the traditional profession of a mystic but has adopted the western dressings, modern scientific gadgets and uses western medicines for the cure of his clients. Almost same is the duality in the character of Pundit Dhaniram in '*The Suffrage of Elvira*'. In case of language too, we notice that Hindi has been so much replaced by English that the East Indians use the latter even in the matters related to religious rites and rituals. Even in '*A House for Mr. Biswas*' when Hari, the family pundit, dies there is no one to take his place as the new generation has received western education and does not opt for the training to become a pundit. Moreover, Mrs. Tulsi's faith yields and she starts following Christian religious rituals and celebrations. This cultural disintegration takes place through a process of seepage and makes itself apparent in their dress codes, food habits and customs. As the inner bastions of the East Indian culture have begun to collapse, there is nothing to fault in the attempts of these protagonists at escaping their existential absurdity and the impending fear of obscurity.

If the western education exerted a corrosive influence on the bastions of East Indian culture from within, the Second World War acted as an external catalyst force in this process of disintegration. It is due to the economic boom precipitated by the American presence in Trinidad that Ganesh in '*The Mystic Masseur*' and Tuttle and Govind in '*A House for Mr. Biswas*' have become prosperous. Ganesh's wife Leela also begins to emulate the externals of the upper class respectability. In '*Miguel Street*' also Edward's dress and mannerism undergo a change soon after he starts working for the Americans. These novels, thus, demonstrate that under the influence of capitalism, people have become worshippers of Mammon and culture and traditions are sacrificed for just pecuniary gains.

As the identity of people rests on their cultural moorings, there is a great crisis in the flux of the postcolonial times. In order to escape from the mediocre environment of the colonial societies whereas Ganesh in '*The Mystic Masseur*' and the omnipresent narrator in '*Miguel Street*' take the escape route to London, the hero of '*A House for Mr. Biswas*' stays back and struggles against the hostile environment and finally succeeds in carving a selfhood. Mr. Bibwas's making of a house is an assertion of his individual identity and this is really a stupendous achievement for a derelict man of his circumstances. Moreover, the earlier novels end on a negative note with their protagonists' rejection and escape but we find that there is an essential positivity in the struggle of Mr. Biswas against the adverse forces. This novel, in a sense, is a social history of three generations of the East Indian immigrants in Trinidad and the hero's struggle to carve out a niche is a symbolic quest of every rootless man to develop an authentic selfhood in exile. On the other hand, the collapse of Tulsi household symbolizes the ultimate breakdown of the insulator of the East Indian community on the alien land. Naipaul adds a fresh insight to the theme of cultural disintegration by demonstrating the widespread confusion in the postcolonial times of the ex-colonies and *'The Suffrage of Elvira'* is its best presentation. In this novel he intends to show how unsuitable the borrowed institution of democracy has proved for the multiracial Trinidad in the era of independence.

After these novels the literary horizon of V.S.Naipaul broadened and he felt a new awareness about his responsibilities as a writer of the postcolonial situations. In 1961 he began his travels from which his future works of fiction as well as non-fiction have emerged. Consequently there is a marked difference in approach, tone and thematic dimensions of the novels written after the author cut across the regional boundaries to secure a place for himself among the writers of the world stream. As the author moves outside and explores other cultures and societies, the recurrent Naipaulian themes of alienation, identity crisis, deracination and mimicry are now viewed in a broader perspective. At the same time these novels, analysed in the fourth chapter of the book, are preoccupied with the broader postcolonial themes of the paradox of freedom, power and the rise of neocolonialism in the emergent nations of the Third World and hence are intensely political documents of the modern times.

'The Mimic Men' sets this forthcoming seriousness and poignancy as it portrays the chaotic situation and paradox of freedom and power in the newly independent colonies. The protagonist of this novel is an exiled political aspirant

fatigued by the disillusion and existential absurdities of the time rather than his failures. Reflections about his failure as a politician lend an insight into the social and political realities of the newly independent countries. The political autobiography of Ralph Singh transcends from the confessional report on an existential allegory in the Third World as the inherent deficiency of the societies in the ex-colonies underlines the illusions, conflicts and vague objectives of their politicians who are only mimic men. Singh's government could not bring about anything positive partly because of the inadequacies of the concerned politicians and greatly because of the deficiencies inherent to the inorganic and half-made society. It is noteworthy that Ralph Singh's quest for identity is more complex because he has to redefine his position in the new socio-political framework. He could attain self-knowledge through the act of writing which brings some order in his otherwise fragmented and disintegrated life.

Naipaul's next novel *'A Flag on the Island'* has a close affinity with *'The Mimic Men'* on the line of theme and structure as both the novels do picturise the widespread chaos and disorder in the newly freed colonies. However, while *'The Mimic Men'* focuses more on the growth and development of the individual politician's selfhood, the latter one provides a panoramic view of the deficient society of the ex- colony. One more noticeable difference is that Ralph Singh is an East Indian member of the society he describes, but Frankie—the first person narrator in *'A Flag on the Island'*, is an American, an outsider observing the miserable predicament of the Caribbean islanders. The mimicry, deficiency and inferiority of the postcolonial societies in the Third World run like a refrain through all the works of Naipaul and this novella reiterates this aspect once again. One more fact is noticed that these second, rather third-rated nations lack local expertise and continue to depend on their imperial patrons for technologies, financial adds and development planning since any sustainable development is impossible as the uncivilized and unskilled people of these invalid societies could not improve themselves to utilize their natural and human resources at all.

'In a Free State' is Naipaul's next novel and here the novelist probes deep into the paradoxical nature of freedom and power in the ex-colonies by setting it in an unnamed African colony. He aims at exposing the dependence syndrome of the colonial people for whom the freedom is just an unbearable burden and mimicry. Instead of being liberated from their parasite existence the colonized peoples have proved themselves only sad casualties of the freedom. It is made quite clear that the colonial mentality of dependence has left these people incapable of shouldering their new-born responsibilities and their freedom has turned into chaos and violence. The title story of this novella focuses on the anarchy that prevails due to internal factions and conflicts which have created almost a civil war like situation. Different violent groups are fighting against each other to seize power in this unruly country of Africa. Majority of the people are shown mindless and violent and after the withdrawal of the colonial powers and their forces these Africans have reverted back to their pre-colonial 'bush life'. This portrayal of the African characters in a totally negative light is a serious limitation of this novelist as in an interview in 1981 with Bharati Mukherjee and Robert Boyers, Naipaul had dismissed Africa as *'a land of bush'*.

Though Naipaul's novels depict the colonial and postcolonial situations at large but *'Guerrillas'* and *'A Bend in the River'* are more vivid and powerful presentations of the violent turmoil and nightmarish experiences in the Third World nations from the point of view of the expatriates living there and so a separate chapter is devoted to these novels in this research analyses. These novels rotate around the theme of political analyses of the contemporary events as well as the complexities of relationship between the colonizers and the colonized. *'Guerrillas'* exposes the sham behind guerrilla movements in the newly independent colonies and opens into what sounds like T.S.Eliot's '*The Waste Land*' inhabited by derelict, immoral and thick headed people. It is clear that inorganic, fragmented and deficient societies can't have any internal source of power as the guerrillas turn out to be disorganized and are mere puppets since the real power is in the hands beyond their sight and visibility. The world picturised in '*Guerrillas*' is on the brink of extinction and this is evident in the Ridge, the city and the commune all of which are described in terms of decay and no one will make a fresh start. The situation further deteriorates in '*A Bend in the River*' as the nihilistic forces unleash violence in all its extremities. Amidst the chaos of the post-independence turmoil the novelist employs the third person omniscient narrator's perspective to dramatize the extremely vulnerable position of the expatriates in an unknown African country which is in the grip of violence and intrigues. The novelist moves in and out of the consciousness of the protagonist Salim—an East Indian Muslim whose group of community and racial people are settled in this continent for generations but they are still rootless derelicts. The prevailing contradictions and malaise in this newly independent African nation are focused through the narrator Salim who has been unnerved by the tribal wars for grappling power. The liberation army's agenda is to exterminate everything and everyone that reminds them of their subjugation.Under the policy of radicalization even the shop of Salim has been taken over and he could escape from the miserable situation only through the help extended by Raymonds. The river—the timeless river—is a silent witness of their agonies and thus shares the making and unmaking of these people on the colonial and postcolonial relics there. Salim's pessimism and existential despair, like that of Naipaul himself, is to some extent temperamental but it is intensified by the negative effects of the rapid political changes and violence all around him. The homelessness, dereliction and nowhereness of the protagonist reflect the predicament experienced by all the immigrants who can never find any final home in their never ending exile. The novel presents a conjuring up of an Indian culture in exile where the immigrants are unable to overcome the nostalgic longings to define or to throw away their lost past.

At the same time Naipaul is skeptical about the new found freedom and progress of Africa and dissents that modernization is another form of mimicry and not only the immigrants but even the natives have to pay for it. The end of '*A Bend in the River*' is also bleak as there is a note of offended transformation and disgust. The political turmoil serves as a backdrop to the tragic drama of the sufferings of the people there. Like a war reporter the novelist effectively reports the tragic vision of the mutilation and fragmentation of the sensibilities of the people amidst violence and disorder. Through the rich arrays of characters Naipaul delineates the gruesome realities in this African nation and the worst affected victims of the post imperial turmoil are the expatriates who have been reduced to non-entity in exile and so are in the miserable status of *'no-land men.'*

This novel again reiterates the fact that Naipaul has made an uncompromising commitment to truth as his deep probing eyes lay bare the malaise of the soul and psyche of the expatriates in this ex-colony of Africa. Naipaul seems to opine that the political independence could offer little hope of change to the Third World societies that have been badly maimed and the imperialistic powers continue to retain their indirect hold there through the newer and more camouflaged methods of the new-colonialism. For instance, the Big Man is only a typical example of the 'Blackman' who has assumed all the lies of the 'Whiteman' in the postcolonial power politics in the Third World countries. Moreover, by depicting the protagonist's journey to London Naipaul has put forward a new dimension of the theme that displacement, alienation and loss of identity are a universal phenomenon in the post Second World War scenario and one must learn to survive with this ultimate truth of the present time. The protagonist of this novel arrives at this wisdom but only after experiencing the ordeal through the hard and harsh ways of the world and his struggle gives a positive message of rejoicing the life as it comes. Therefore, in spite of the pessimistic vision, the human concern makes this novel more powerful one compared to *'Guerrillas'*.

Naipaul's works offer little hope to the Third World societies that have been damaged beyond any hope of repair and in the post-independence situation life has been reduced to sheer fluidity without any authentic foothold at all. The nervous breakdown of Biswas, the morbid despair and sadness of Ralph Singh and Salim are the tainting influences of the colonial experiences on the soul and psyche of the Third World people. It will not be any exaggeration to say that every hero of these novels has acquired a wisdom of self-appraisal and insight to take the positive faith in himself. This positivity becomes the testament of the new philosophy to face the world without any grudge any more. However, '*A Bend in the River*' concludes with Naipaul's failure to arrive at any positive conclusion about Africa which, according to him, is a land of bush.

Even emotional and sexual intimacy is dominated by the bleak tendency of materialistic or political motifs to such an extent that all the man- woman relations end in misogynist violence, perversion and desolate situations. Thus, the fragmentation and desolation, both at the macrocosmic level of the society as well as the microcosmic level of the individual, act as aggressive deterrent to stability and growth in the era of globalization.

Naipaul's inability to identify with India makes him realize this homelessness and identity crisis of the Indian immigrants as an existential absurdity, but in his later novels, covered in the sixth chapter, these problems of displacement, dereliction and homelessness are realized as a universal phenomenon of modern times. Now, he seems to suggest that fluidity of existence and exile are the harsh realities of the postcolonial era as the whole world is in the grip of turmoil and upheaval and there is no promising land—not even England—the land of the white masters, or America—

the land of all growth and power that can give any shelter or solace and so one has to learn to cope with the prevailing oddities and challenges. Even the past could offer no consolation in the new emerging wilderness of the world and so it is necessary to inculcate a capacity to trample on the past and be audacious enough to survive in the world and accept it as it is. Naipaul himself shares this agony and ordeal of the immigrants as he proclaims in '*The Enigma of Arrival*': **"There was no ship of antique shape now to take us back. We had to come out of the nightmare and there was nowhere else to go."**[2] This powerful travelogue, presenting the marvelous admixture of autobiographical facts and psychological fiction, records Naipaul's conscious journey from one place to another, from the British colony of Trinidad to the countryside of England and from one state of mind to another. Naipaul's own pain of being a non-entity with a dead-ended past and uncertain future distressed him and ultimately resulted in conditioning him to find a liberated writer within himself during the 'sojourn' in a changed surroundings in English countryside. This celebrated travel-fiction articulates persistent search, the ambivalent feelings and painful self-laceration of the novelist. Thus the curse of Naipaul's homelessness turned into a disguised boon in his solitude and by shedding away the weak and jangling nerves of being a stranger he procured a sagacity to harness himself to rejoice the never ending exile. The novel can be described as a record of the metamorphosis of this prolific dissenter who wipes away from his sensibility the weird impressions of the wounds caused by the wreckage of history—if he could—as he records, without rancour or nostalgia, the new contemplations of time with a self- ordained vision and voice. His new contemplation forced Naipaul to look on displacement, on disintegration, on alienation, on exile and on death as the new truths of the mysterious human existence and this novel concludes with wonderment and a conviction to deal with these truths at large.

This autobiographical work could also be seen as an advanced re-writing of '*A House for Mr. Biswas*' since both the novels are a journey towards self-realisation and self-assertion to find an authentic selfhood and both do culminate in achievement of the same. Moreover, the first half of both ends in failure. The narrator's return to Wiltshire reminds us of Mr. Biswas returning to Port of Spain in utter dejection to the Tulsi house with an intention to rejuvenate for a new start once again. Biswas's story ends in building a house, the young narrator's ordeal culminates in finding a new self-reliant writer with the thundering force of truthfulness. Thus out of 'nowhereness' emerges 'everywhereness' and for Naipaul this obvious victory is the great landmark in Diaspora sensibility to celebrate their exile. This continuity and innovative progress in thematic perception justifies Naipaul's own proclamation that all his works are inter-related and may be treated as a big book.

Naipaul' view about culture is progressive but a vigilant reader of his novels can't forget to note a recurrent regret on the passing away and colossal loss of the old order. Moreover, a few years ago, after famously declaring the sad demise of the much exhausted novel and also openly labeling India as a historical darkness having no autonomous and sustainable life, Naipaul has again, with India on his mind, made a remarkable comeback with his novel *'Half a Life'* in 2001 followed by its extension *'Magic Seeds'* in 2004. In spite of all his defiant denunciation of India, we find Naipaul quite open and honest in delineating the truth that he could not free himself from the haunting shadow of his ancestral land. For example, in *'Half a Life'* he has used India as a fictional material and he appears to overcome his demonstrably wrong and angry indictments in his works like *'An Area of Darkness'* and *'India; A Million Mutinies Now'*.

'Half a Life' is once again preoccupied with Naipaul's favourite theme of immigrant's identity crisis and search for a new face in the mirror of time by negating the root image. It is rather surprising that here the protagonist—son of a Brahmin man and a low caste woman—is born in India and his disintegration and alienation begins at home and ends

in his vain search for some alternate face even if that is fiend. As a champion of the theme of the socio-cultural crises in limbo Naipaul reiterates the adverse consequences of this attempt and in this novel it is Willie Somerset Chandran who is the central figure on a tragic quest for some alternate identity. So *'Half a Life'* re-endorses the fact that the past of the immigrants is though merely a shadow yet, one can't betray it and in the vain attempt to erase the past one only stakes one's present and future as well. Willie's desperate attempt to run away from his ignoble parental background and even his half-life as an Indian of mixed caste is completely dissolved in his bohemian existence abroad. Self-hatred and negation of his roots reduces Willie to a *'sojourner'* rather to a *'nowhere man'*. It is ironically tragic that in his defiant search to find some new respectable face Willie sets another much more complicated and faceless mould for himself and later on he realizes the seriousness of these repercussions caused by the rebounds of the past. In his efforts to wipe away the stigma of guilty parentage, Willie floats in the wilderness of exiled life in the West and procures nothing. Thus, this novel portrays a surpassing emotional conflict, an agony of half-ness and a futile search of a forlorn Indian for El Dorado in West which leads nowhere. The break from the past pushes Willie into a flux that keeps him dangling for many painful years before he earns the wisdom to realize that it is high time to stop making a fool of himself.

Whereas, *'The Enigma of Arrival'* picturises Naipaul's own conflict and crisis and his ultimate growth as a writer with a liberator soul, *'Half a Life'* must be judged as coming of age and wisdom to Naipaul's progressive heroes who endeavour to survive and carve their niche in limbo and it again reiterates the connectivity and continuity thread in his novels. Willie in Naipaul's twelfth novel may, in many ways, be different from Ganesh in *'The Mystic Masseur'*, Biswas in *'A House for Mr. Biswas'* and Ralph Singh in *' The Mimic Men'* but basically and essentially they all are the faces of one figure 'an Indian Immigrant in limbo' and therefore, present the different stages of the great search for authenticity and also for a wisdom to cope with their existence in exile. So Naipaul's literary works derive their strength from the writer's own life and his resolution to carve a new giant image in the mirror of time is shared by his heroes in his fiction. It is, however, equally surprising that by presenting an India born protagonist in '*Half a Life*' Naipaul seems to share the vicarious longings of this hero for his lost past i. e. 'Indianness'. Perhaps, this realization of the nativity led this prolific dissenter to proclaim in 2004 that he could not reject India and even feels happy by recollecting this reality. It is equally noteworthy that though Naipaul has all admiration for the positive features of the West yet, at the same time, he is very clear-sighted and emphatic about his own distance from it. This fact is quite justified by Naipaul's proclamation in his interview with Ian Hamilton in 1971 in London as: **"London is my metropolitan centre; it is my commercial centre; and yet I know that it is a kind of limbo and that I am a refugee in the sense that I am always peripheral. One's concerns are not the concerns of local people."**[3]

Actually Naipaul is relentless in speaking the truths and in his delineation he is like an honest surgeon exposing the malaise of the people all around the world. Moreover, the brutal analysis of the post-colonial complexities of the Third World societies as well as the miserable predicament of the immigrants is a kind of shock-treatment which, he believes, is necessary to pull them out of their complacency and make them shoulder their responsibilities towards themselves in the present scenario. The corrosive influence of the materialism and the disgusting desolation has resulted in widespread despair and fear-psychosis lest their identity be swallowed in such oppressive situations and herein lies the root cause of their malaise. It will not be any exaggeration to say that every relation is experienced as a version of the binary of Domination versus Subordination and the prevalent corruption and exploitation precludes any intimacy in human relationship.

Naipaul presents the realistic phenomenon as the people, especially of the Third World, are facing the crises of social orphanage and their lives are now out of their grip and gear as symbolized by the protagonists of his novels at large. His masterly craftsmanship lies in the fact that he has presented the heroes in all their littleness and has still preserved the universality of the theme by making them the representatives of all the displaced and derelicts across the seven seas. In Naipaul's view the Indian way of perception is mostly negative because the Indians—whether living in their own country or the immigrants floating on the alien lands—are quite deficient in facing the situations in the aftermath of the colonial reign as they **"do not directly explore the world; rather they are defined by it."**[4] Naipaul seems to suggest that the society of the East Indians in exile has lost its essence beyond any hope of revival and the people have been reduced to homeless dwellers and derelicts with no sense of belongingness and they are in a malaise of no land man. He suggests that there is no promising land—not even England or America—that can give them any shelter or solace and one has to learn to cope with the prevailing situation. Moreover, the nostalgic remembrance of the past glory could offer no consolation in the new emerging wilderness of the world. Naipaul holds this defect of vision to be ultimately responsible for their intellectual deficiency, desperate search for some alternate identity and marginalization. That is why he exhorts that, **"the past has to be seen to be dead, or the past will kill."**[5] The greatest strength of this relentless author is the wisdom he wants to convey to the Third World people by these exhortations for self-assertion and self-reliance through audacious explorations of the world without making grudges or lame excuses any more.

In Naipaul's oeuvre the process of writing is seen to be a progressing creative endeavour leading to self- knowledge and nourishment of the sensibility to survive amidst the oddities of the postcolonial situations of the world. It is, therefore, obvious that self-actualisation, audacity and self-appraisal are the answers to the people of the Third World either in their own country or in their floating existence as ever exiled immigrants on any patch of the earth. It is only then that their cultural parasitism and second-rated intellectual status could be removed and their decolonization in its real sense could be possible and this operation is a must to free them from all the stressing pressures of their wrecked past culture and distorted identity. The expatriates in limbo can become integrated identity only if they recognize and realize this truth of their existential despair and fluidity of life.

Along with exhorting his people to be brave to decolonize themselves, Naipaul proclaims that he has decolonized himself in his own peculiar way i.e., through the process of creative exposition of his observations as well as his lived experiences across the world. In this regard he declared as:

> ".........I've decolonized myself through the practice of writing, through what I've learned from writing, looking at the world, But let me also add to this I feel an enormous pain about the situation."[6]

Fortunately, Naipaul himself has procured a wisdom to look on life, on death, on man and on all human existence in modern world as a mystery which is equally baffling to each and every man and this self-ordained realization has harnessed him with a Ulysses-like power of looking at life and the world in a new perspective. This philosophy of V. S. Naipaul is encapsulated in the opening sentence in '*A Bend in the River*' quoted at in the beginning of this concluding chapter and this powerful proclamation '*World Is What It Is*'[7] has become the title of V. S. Naipaul's confessional biography by London-based English writer Patrick French who has been credited with his critically-acclaimed bare-all tone on Nobel Laureate's life. In this confessional record Naipaul is extraordinarily audacious as he reveals everything whether it was moral, amoral or immoral in the perspective of the worldly code of conduct.

This broadening of Naipaul's vision and wisdom enriched

his literary sensibility to exhort the immigrants to celebrate their exiled status with no longing lingering look behind and herein lies his indispensible greatness as a giant and high profile writer whose works have become a landmark in the annals of the Diaspora literature. Taking an overview of Naipaul's contribution to the postcolonial literature we may conclude that his position as a writer of an international repute and universal appeal is accentuated because his works have become the paradigms of the entire modern world's experiences of exile, desolation, dereliction, deracination and floating existence. So far as the question of his own lack of roots is concerned, Naipaul has converted this weakness into his strength and also into a weapon with which he could slice up the countries or the societies he visits. This power of his works has attributed Naipaul a high profile as an unforgiving and relentlessly truthful and somehow narcissistic dissenter of the present time all over the world.

References

1. *A Bend in the River, op. cit.*, p. 3.
2. *The Enigma of Arrival, op. cit.*, p. 385.
3. V. S. Naipaul; Without a Place, 'Critical Perspectives' by Ian Hamilton, *Times Literary Supplement*, 30 July 1971, p. 41.
4. V. S. Naipaul, *India: A Wounded Civilization*, (New Delhi: Penguin 1979), p. 103.
5. Ibid., p. 174.
6. V. S. Naipaul, 'Portrait of An Artist: What makes Naipaul Run', by Roul Pantin, *Caribbean Contact*, 1.6 (1973), p. 18.
7. Patrick French, *The World Is What It Is*: Confessional Biography of V.S.Naipaul.(London: Andre Deutsch, 2007, Harmondsworth: Penguin Books, 2007).

Bibliography

PRIMARY SOURCES

FICTION

Naipaul, V.S. : *The Mystic Masseur.* London : Picador—an imprint of Pan Macmillan Ltd., 2002. (First Published in 1957).

.... : *The Suffrage of Elvira.* Harmondsworth : Penguin Books, 1969. (First Published in 1958).

.... : *Miguel Street.* London; Picador—an imprint of Pan Macmillan Ltd., 2005. (First Published in 1961).

.... : *A House for Mr. Biswas.* London: Picador—an imprint of Pan Macmillan Ltd.,2005. (First Published in 1961).

.... : *Mr. Stone and the Knight's Companion.* London; Andre Deutsch,1963.

.... : *The Mimic Men.* Harmondsworth: Penguin Books, 1983. (First Published in 1967).

.... : *A Flag on the Island.* London: Andre Deutsch, 1967.

.... : *In a Free State.* London: Andre Deutsch,1971. Harmondsworth: Penguin Books,1969.

.... : *Guerrillas.* London: Andre Deutsch,1975. Harmondsworth: Penguin Books, 1976.

.... : *A Bend in the River*. London: Picador—an imprint of Pan Macmillan Ltd., 2002.(First Published in 1979).

Naipaul, V. S. : *The Enigma of Arrival*. London: Picador – an imprint of Pan Macmillan Ltd.,2002. (First Published in 1987).

.... : *A Way in the World*. London: Andre Deutsch, 1994.

.....................: *Half A Life*. London: Picador—an imprint of Pan Macmillan Ltd., 2001.

NON-FICTION

Naipaul, V. S. : *The Middle Passage*. London: Andre Deutsch, 1962. Harmondsworth: Penguin Books, 1969.

.... : *An Area of Darkness*. London: Andre Deutsch, 1964. New Delhi: Penguin Books, 1968.

.... : *The Loss of El Dorado*. London: Andre Deutsch, 1969.

.... : *The Overcrowded Barracoon and Other Articles*. London: Andre Deutsch,1972. Harmondsworth: Penguin Books: 1976.

.... : *India : A Wounded Civilization*. London: Andre Deutsch, 1977. New Delhi: Penguin Books,1979.

.... : *The Return of Eva Peron with the Killings in Trinidad*. New York: Alfred A. Knopf, 1980. Harmondsworth: Penguin Books,1981.

.... : *Among the Believers*. London: Andre Deutsch,1981. Harmondsworth: Penguin Books, 1982.

.... : *Finding the Centre: Two Narratives*. London: Andre Deutsch,1984. Harmondsworth; Penguin Books, 1985.

.... : *A Turn in the South*. New York: Vintage Books, 1989. London: Picador—an imprint of Pan Macmillan Ltd., 2003.

.... : *India : A Million Mutinies Now.* London: Minerva,1990. London: Vintage Books, 1998.

.... : *Beyond Belief: Islamic Excursions Among the Converted Peoples.* London: Vintage Books, 1998.

LETTERS

Naipaul, V. S. : *Letters Between a Father and Son.* London: Abacus, 1999. London: Picador—an imprint of Pan Macmillan Ltd., 2002.

ARTICLES

Naipaul, V. S. : ' London', *Times Literary Supplement,* 15 August,1958.

.... : 'Speaking of Writing', *Times,* 2 Jan.1964:11.

.... : 'The Writer' , Critical Perspectives, Ed. Robert D. Hamner. London: Heinmann,1977; 30-33.

.... : ' Writing A House for Mr. Biswas'. *New York Review of Books.* 24 Nov. 1983: 22-23.

.... : 'Returning to Centre'. *The Sunday Express,* New Delhi: 16 Sept. 2007. 3.

INTERVIEWS

Naipaul, V.S. : *'Interview with Francis Wyndham'.* Sunday Times, 10 Sept. 1968: 24.

.... : ' Without a Place', by Ian Hamilton. *Times Literary Supplement.* 30 July, 1971: 897-898.

..................:' The Novelist V.S. Naipaul Talks to Nigel Bingham About his Childhood in Trinidad'. *Listener,* 7 Sept. 1972: 306.

.... : ' V.S. Naipaul: A Transition Interview by Adrian Rowe Evans'. *Transition.* Dec. 1971. Rept. in *Quest.* (Poona) Sept. Oct. 1972: 47-55.

.... : 'Portrait of An Artist' : What Makes Naipaul Run'. Roaul Pantin. *Caribbean Contact,* 1.6 (1973): 15, 18-19.

.... : 'It's Everyman For Himself': V.S. Naipaul on India'. By Charles Wheeler. *Listener,* 27 Oct. 1977; 535-537.

.... : 'V.S. Naipaul; Man Without Society'. By Shankar Israel. New York Times; Book Review. 7 Oct. 1971.

.... : 'People are Proud of Being Stupid'. *Newsweek,* 18 Aug. 1980: 38.

Naipaul, V.S. : ' A Conversation With V.S. Naipaul'. By Robert Boyers and Bharati Mukherjee, *Salmagundi,* 54, 1981: 6.

.... : 'India has Vitality'. By Rahul Singh. *India Today,* 31 July 1989 : 120.

.... : 'An Area of Awakening: V.S. Naipaul in Conversation With Dileep Padgaonkar'. *The Sunday Times of India,* 18 July, 1993.

.... : 'Delivering the Truth.' *Times Literary Supplement,* 2 Sept. 1994: 3-4.

SECONDARY SOURCES

CRITICAL BOOKS

Amar, G.S. and : *Colonial Consciousness in Common Wealth*
S.K. Desai, eds. *Literature.*_Bombay: Somaya Publication. 1984.

Barnouw, Dagmar. : *Naipaul's Strangers.* Bloomington & Indianapolis: Indiana University Press. 2003.

Bhat, Yashoda. : *V.S. Naipaul: An Introduction.* New World Literature 118. Delhi: B.R. Publishing Corporation, 1999.

Boehmer, Elleke. : *Colonial and Post- Colonial Literature: Migrant Metaphors.* Oxford: Oxford University Press.1997.

Boxill, Anthony. : *V.S. Naipaul's Fiction: In Quest of the Enemy.* Frederiction, New Brunswick: York Press, 1993.

Cesaire, Aime. : *Discourse on Colonialism.* New York : Monthly Review Press, 1972.

Cohn, Bernard S. : *Colonialism and its Forms of Knowledge: The British in India.* Delhi: Oxford University Press, 1997.

Cudjoe, Selwyn S. : *V.S. Naipaul: A Materialist Reading.* Amherst: The University of Massachusetts Press, 1988.

Eagleton, Terry. : *Exiles And Emigres.* London: Chatto and Windus, 1970.

.... : *Studies in a Dying Colonialism. 1989.* Harmondsworth: Penguin Books, 1970.

Feder, Lilian. :*Naipaul's Truth.* New Delhi : Indialog Publications, 2001.

French, Patrick. *'The World is What it is'.* Confessional Biography of V.S. Naipaul. London: Andre Deutsch: 2007. Harmondsworth: Penguin Books, 2007.

Goonatilake,Sushanta. : *Crippled Minds : An Exploration into Colonial Culture.* Bombay: Vikas, 1982.

Gowda, Anniah H.H. ed. : *The Colonial and Neo-Colonial Encounters in Commonwealth Literature.* Mysore: Mysore University Press, 1983.

Gurr, Andrew. : *Writers in Exile : The Creative Use of Home in Modern Literature.* Sussex: The Harvester Press, 1981.

Hamner, Robert D. ed. : *Critical Perspectives on V.S. Naipaul.* London: Heinmann, 1979.

Hayward, Helen.: *The Enigma of V.S. Naipaul: Sources and Context.* New York: Palgrave Macmillan, 2002.

Hermassi, Elbaki. : *The Third World Reassessed.* Berkeley: University of California Press,1980.

Hughes, Peter. : *V.S. Naipaul: Contemporary Writers.* London: Routledge, 1988.

Joshi, Chandra B. : *V.S. Naipaul: The Voice of Exile.* Delhi: Sterling Publishers, 1994.

Kamra, Shashi. : *The Novels of V.S. Naipaul.* New Delhi: Prestige Publishers, 1990.

King, Bruce. : *West Indian Literature.* London: Macmillan, 1979.

Lamming, George. : *In the Castle of My Skin.* London: Longman Drumbeat, 1979.

.... : *The Pleasures of Exile.* London: Michael Joseph, 1960.

Loomba, Ania.: *Colonialism/ Post-colonialism.* London: Rontledge,1998.

Memmi, Albert. : *The Colonizer and the Colonized.* London: Earthscan, 1990.

Mohan, Champa Rao. : *Postcolonial Situation in the Novels of V.S. Naipaul.* New Delhi: Atlantic Publishers And Distributors, 2004.

Moore, Gerald. : *The Chosen Tongue: English Writing in the Tropical World.* London: Longman, 1969.

Nandy, Ashis. : *The Intimate Enemy: Loss and Recovery of Self Under Colonialism.* New Delhi: Oxford University Press, 1983.

Narsimhaiah, C. D. ed. : *Awakened Conscience : Studies in Commonwealth Literature.* New Delhi: Sterling Publication, 1978.

.... : *The Critical Indian Scene : Controversial Essays.* Delhi: B.R. Publishing Corp. 1990.

Newson, Linda A. : *Aboriginal and Spanish Colonial Trinidad: A Study in Cultural Contact.* London; Academic Press, 1976.

Panwar, Purabi. ed.: *V.S. Naipaul: An Anthology of Recent Criticism.* Delhi: Pencraft International,2003.

Rai, Sudha. : *V.S. Naipaul: A Study in Expatriate Sensibility.* New Delhi : Arnold Heinmann,1982.

Ramadevi, N. : *The Novels of V.S. Naipaul : Quest for Order and Identity.* New Delhi: Prestige, 1996.

Rao, Madhusudan K.I. : *Contrary Awareness : A Critical Study* of the Novels of V.S.Naipaul. Guntur : Saradhi, 1982.

Ray, Mohit K. ed.: *V.S. Naipaul: Critical Essays, Vol.1&2*. New Delhi : Atlantic Publishers and Distributors, 2002.

Singh, Manjit Inder. : *V.S. Naipaul: Writers of the Indian Diaspora.* Jaipur; Rawat Publications, 1998.

Suleri, Sara. : *The Rhetoric of English in India.* Chicago : University of Chicago Press, 1992.

Theroux, Paul. : *V.S. Naipaul : An Introduction to His Works.* London: Andre Deutsch, 1972.

Walsh, William. ed. : *A Manifold Voice : Studies in Commonwealth Literature.* London: Chatto and Windus, 1970.

.... : *Readings in Commonwealth Literature.* Oxford: The Clarendon Press,1973.

.... : *V.S. Naipaul, The Modern Writers' Series.* Edinburgh: Oliver and Boyd, 1973.

William, Eric.: *History of the People of Trinidad and Tobago.* London; Andre Deutsch, 1964.

ARTICLES

Anderson, Linda R. : "Ideas of Identity and Freedom in V.S. Naipaul And Joseph Conrad". *English Studies,* 59 (1978): 510-17.

Angrosino, M.B. : "V.S. Naipaul and the Colonial Image". *Caribbean Quarterly,* 21.3 (1975) : 1-11.

Bellit, Ben. : "The Heraldry of Accommodation : A House for Mr. Naipaul". *Salmagundi,* 54 (1981): 22-24.

Birje-Patil, J. : "From Heart of Darkness to a Free State". *Colonial Consciousness in Commonwealth Literature.* eds. G.S. Amar and S.K. Desai.110-118.

Boxill, Anthony. : V.S. Naipaul's Starting Point". *Journal of Commonwealth Literature.* 10.1 (1975): 1-9.

.... : " Mr. Biswas,Mr. Polly and the Problem of V.S. Naipaul's Sources". *Ariel,* 8.3 (1977) : 129-141.

Carthew, John. : "Adapting to Trinidad: Mr. Biswas and Mr. Polly Revisited". *Journal of Commonwealth Literature.* 13.1 (1978) : 58-64.

Choubey, Asha. : "A Critique of Naipaul's Half a Life: Searching for Identity in Limbo".*V.S. Naipaul: Critical Essays,* Vol. 1, Ed. Mohit K. Ray. New Delhi : Atlantic Publishers and Distributors (2002): 226-237.

.... : " Naipaul's Half a Life: Coming to Terms with King Cophetua". *V.S. Naipaul: Critical Essays,* Vol.2. Ed. Mohit K. Ray. New Delhi : Atlantic Publishers and Distributors (2002); 166-175.

Chakraborti,Santosh. : "Naipaul's Discourse of Aspiration : A Study of *'Mystic Masseur'* and *' A House for Mr.Biswas"*. *V.S. Naipaul: Critical Essays,* Vol. 1. Ed. Mohit K. Ray. New Delhi: Atlantic Publishers And Distributors, (2002) : 30-45.

Dalrymple, William. : "An Aria of Darkness : Naipaul's New Book Traverses Old Ground". *Outlook,* New Delhi: 24 Sept. 2007: 80-81.

Derrick, A.C. : "Naipaul's Technique as a Novelist". *Critical Perspectives,* Ed. Hamner. 194-206.

Dhondy, Farrukh. : V.S. Naipaul : An Unrepentant Writer". *The Times of India.* New Delhi:Monday, 24 Sept. 2007.

Hamner, R.D. : "Character and Setting". *Critical Perspectives on V.S. Naipaul* (London: 1979). 205-241.

Harit, Satish K. : "V.S. Naipaul and Indian Psyche". *V.S. Naipaul: Critical Essays,* Vol. 2. Ed. Mohit K. Ray. New Delhi: Atlantic Publishers and Distributors (2002): 76-84.

Kundu, Rama. : 'An Indian Who is Not an Indian". *V.S. Naipaul: Critical Essays,* Vol. 1. Ed. Mohit K. Ray. New Delhi: Atlantic Publishers and Distributors (2002): 119-148.

Langran, Phillip. : "V.S. Naipaul : A Question of Detachment". *Journal of Commonwealth Literature .25.1* (1990) : 133-141.

MacDonald, Bruce F. : "Symbolic Action in Three of V.S. Naipaul's Novels". *Critical Prespectives.* Ed. R.D. Hamner. 242-254.

Maini, Darshan Singh. : "The Complex Fate of V.S. Naipaul". *Colonial Consciousness in Commonwealth Literature.* Eds. G.S. Amar and S.K. Desai. 93-109.

Mann, Harveen Sachdeva. : "Variations on the Theme of Mimicry:Naipaul's *The Mystic Masseur* and *The Suffrage of Elvira*". *Modern Fiction Studies.* 30.3 (1984): 467-485.

Mukherjee, Meenakshi. : "Caliban's Growth: Impact of Colonialism On Commonwealth Fiction". *Colonial Consciousness in Commonwealth Literature.* Ed. G.S. Amar and S.K. Deasi. 216-227.

Nachman, Larry David : "The Worlds of V.S. Naipaul". *Salmagundi.* 54 (1981): 59-76.

Nandan, Kavita. : "Exile in *The Mimic Men*". *V.S. Naipaul; An Anthology of Recent Criticism.* Ed. Purabi Panwar. Delhi: Pencraft International (2002): 126-143.

Ormerod, David. : "In a Derelict Land : The Novels of V.S. Naipaul". *Critical Perspectives.* Ed. Hamner. 159-177.

Padhi, Babhu. : "Naipaul on Naipaul and the Novel". *Modern Fiction Studies.* 30.3 (1984): 455-465.

Prasannarajan, S. : "V.S. Naipaul; The Provocateur". *India Today.* Delhi: 10 Sept. 2007: 54-64.

Prescott, Lynda. : "Past and Present Darkness: Sources for V.S. Naipaul's *A Bend in the River*". *Modern Fiction Studies.* 30.3 (1984): 547-559.

Rama, Devi N. : "Naipaul's *The Mimic Men*: Order and Form Through Art". *V.S. Naipaul: Critical Essays.* Vol. 2. Ed. Mohit K.Ray. New Delhi: Atlantic Publishers and Distributors. (2002): 30-45.

Rao,K.I. Madhusudan. : "V.S.Naipaul's Guerrillas:A Fable of political Innocence and Experience". *Journal of Commonwealth Literature.* 14.1 (1979): 90-99.

Rohlehr, Gordon. : "The Ironic Approach: The Novels of V.S. Naipaul".*Critical Perspectives.* Ed. Hamner. 178- 193.

Sen, Ashoke. : "*Miguel Street* and *Half a Life:* A Study in Contrast". *V.S. Naipaul: Critical Essays.* Vol. 1. Ed. Mohit K. Ray. New Delhi: Atlantic Publishers & Distributors (2002): 238-247.

Sharpe, Jenny. : "Figures of Colonial Resistance". *Modern Fiction Studies.* 35.1 (1989): 137-179.

Singh, Veena. : "Paradox of Freedom in *A Bend in the River*". *V.S. Naipaul : Critical Essays,* Vol. 2. eEd. Mohit K. Ray. New Delhi: Atlantic Publishers and Distributors (2002): 123-134.

Srinath, C.N. : "Crisis of Identity: Assertion and Withdrawal in Naipaul and Arun Joshi". *Literary Criterion.* 14.1 (1979): 33-41.

Theroux, Paul. : 'V.S. Naipaul". *Modern Fiction Studies.* 30.3 (1984) : 339-343.

Thieme, John. : "V.S. Naipaul's Third World: A Not So Free State". *Journal of Commonwealth Literature,*10.1 (1975): 10-12.

Vijayasree, S.& T. Vijay Kumar. : "A House for Mr. Naipaul". *Iaclals Newsletter.* Jan. 2002.

Walsh, William. : "V.S. Naipaul : Mr. Biswas". *Literary Criterion.* 10.2 (1972): 27-37.

Wirth-Nesher, Hanna. : "The Curse of Marginality Colonialism in Naipaul's *Guerrillas*". *Modern Fiction Studies.* 30.3 (1984): 531-545.

Woodcock, George. : "Two Great Commonwealth Novelists: R.K. Narayan and V.S. Naipaul". *Sewanee Review.* 87 (1979): 1-28.

Wyndham, Frances. : "V.S. Naipaul". *Listener.* 7 Oct. 1971.

Index

A

A bend in the river, 28, 101, 116-17, 125, 137, 139, 185, 191
A community without rule, 124
A flag on the Island, 96, 181
A house for Mr. Biswas, 26, 41, 59, 73, 78, 95, 152, 185, 191
A land of bush, 182
A money crouch, 24
A second Diaspora, 23
A writer's people ways of seeing and feeling, 35
An area of darkness, 4-5, 20, 34, 82-83, 86, 187
Africa saved my life, 107
Aldous Husley, 3
Among the believer! An Islamic journey, 37
Ancient marinhar (the), 169
Ana's London man, 168
Anglophile, 14
Area of darkness 14
Au..nor's own life, 144

B

Beyond belief: Islamic excursions among the converted papers, 37
Big man, 134
Bigger maid, 161
British crown, 172
Bush life, 182

B

Caribbean
  countries, 2
  islands, 10
  origin like Derek, 13
  own father Seeparsad, 13
Christianity, 104
Circus at Luxor (the), 110
Colonial
  anglophile, 32
  myth, 173
  Trinidad, 8

view, 108
Commonwealth literature, 33
Compound wives, 106
Contrary awareness: A critical study of the novels of V.S. Naipaul, 34
Cripple Villi, 92
Cultural disintegration and immigrants quest, 40
Cultural-ideological mind, 155

D

Daily telegraph (the), 9
Dayo's
brothers, 104
failure, 105
Delivering the truth, 154
Denis Williams, 5
Diaspora identity across, 143
Difficult, 119

E

East Indian
immigrants, 26
Nazruddin Mahesh, 128
Elvira, you is a bitch, 53
Enigma of arrival (the), 30-31, 83, 144, 148-49, 152-53, 169, 188
Ex-colonies, 115-16
Exiled novelists, 20
existential despairy, 115
Experience, 155
Experience of Diapora, 3

F

Father Huisman's killing, 131
Fictions Canadian father, 161
Finding the centre, 24, 154
Fluidity of life, 115

G

Gandhi's call, 159
Girmitya, 149, 174
Grappling, 128
Guerridas, 28, 116-18, 124, 135, 138-39, 182-83

H

Half a life, 31, 157, 168, 187-89
Half-rebel Brahmin, 158
Heterogeneous and fragmented society of Trinidad, 22
Highly combustible, 119
Hindu norms of *Karma, Dharma* and Moksha, 34
Hughes's study concentrates, 33

I

In a free state, 28, 101, 106, 108, 110, 182
India
A million mutinies now, 14, 30, 187
A wounded civilization, 4, 14, 30
Indian diaspora, 13

Indianness, 178

J

Jack's large house, 146
Jimmy's half-cast status, 124
Journey, an emphatic singular, 144

K

King cophetua, 161
Kripalville, 92

L

Little gidding, 148
Loss of El Dorado (the), 28

M

Magic seeds, 31, 38
Ma, I am going to make body, 58
Middle passage, 11, 14, 27, 55, 78, 80-81
Miguel street (the), 41, 58, 178-79
Mimic men (the), 27, 86, 88-89, 95-96, 111, 117, 180
Mr. stone and the knight's companion, 27, 87
Mystic masseur (the), 26, 41, 46, 48, 88, 157, 170, 178, 188

N

Naipaul, V.S., 1, 3
Naipaul's
  ancestral origin, 12
  artistic vision, 33
  attempt to understand, 32
  childhood and ever since, 83
  development, 33
  entire, 3
  final phase, 31
  guesto, 25
  important novels, 17
  judgementr on India, 34
  life and experiences, 21
  literature originated form, 4
  literary career, 25
  masterly craftmanship, 74
  prediament in India, 84
  rejection, 8
  response 'I am not a cricketer' 16
  truth, 138
  vision and sensibility, 19, 21
  works revolve, 16
New Statesman, 9
New World 22
No land's man 147, 184
Non-fictional form, 23
Novel portrays, 26
Nowhere man, 188

O

One out of many, 102
Orlando pattern, 5
Ostensibly working, 119

Our universal civilization, 30
Outsider, 10
Overcrowded Baracoon, 28

P

Paradox of freedom, 78
Petricia Anne Hap, 10
Pleasure of exile (the), 34
Post-colonial era, 115
Post-colonial chaos, 78
Post-colonial literature, 2
Post-independence situations, 116, 158
Post-World War, 1
Power in the third world nations, 78
Prasannarajan, N., compliment, 13

R

Ramayan, 22, 54
Ramp, 156
Remove, 155
Return of Evaparon with the killings in Trinidad, 28

S

Salim, 126
Salim's pessimism and existential, 129
Savage, 108
Sever, seas, 193
Sing's
  gesture of rebellion, 92
  government, 181
  various failures, 89
Socialist (the), 94
Sojourner, 162, 188
State domain, 132
Story, 13
Suffrage of Elvira (the), 26, 41, 47, 52, 54, 178, 180
Summing-up, 172

T

Tell me who to kill, 104, 106
Third world, 126, 190
Third world nations, 115-16, 175
Third world countries, 2, 10, 17, 26
Third world reassessed, 20
Thrush cross grange 120, 124
Trinidad—the Caribbean, 12
Trinidad society, 15
Truthful artist, 12
Typical colonies anglophile, 20

U

Uncreative, 23

W

Wast land (the), 119
Watching the film, 122

West Indian traidition, 24
Whiteman's burden (the), 173
Wider process, 3
Wild free state, 107
Willie chandran, 161
Willie's
  blood, 159
  defiant soul, 160
  identify leads, 160
  question, 160
  second composition, 161
  social cultural, 159
Wuthering heights, 124

Y

Young caribbean poet, 16
Yveta, 126

Z

Zabeth, 126, 131
Zaire and places, 129
Zigzagging, 156
Zulu youth, 107